CYRIL W. BEAUMONT

By the same author

Ninette de Valois: Idealist without Illusions
De Basil's Ballets Russes
Eyes on the Ballet
Eyes on Mime
Dance and its Creators
Brief for Ballet
Robert Helpmann
Ballet for Boys and Girls (with Joan Butler)
The Royal Ballet: a Picture History (with Sarah C. Woodcock)
Writings on Dance 1938-68 by A.V. Coton
(edited with Lilian Haddakin)

Cyril Beaumont at the door of his bookshop, 75 Charing Cross Road, London.

CYRIL W. BEAUMONT
Dance writer and publisher

Kathrine Sorley Walker

DANCE BOOKS

First published in 2006 by Dance Books Ltd
The Old Bakery, 4 Lenten Street,
Alton, Hampshire GU34 1HG
Copyright © Kathrine Sorley Walker

ISBN 1 85273 110 9

A CIP catalogue record for this book
is available from the British Library

Printed and bound in Great Britain by
Latimer Trend and Company Ltd, Plymouth, Devon

Acknowledgements

The material in this book originally appeared in slightly different form in the scholarly journal *Dance Chronicle*. The author and publisher would like to thank the editors of *Dance Chronicle*, Jack Anderson and George Dorris, for their assistance in making the material available in book form. The *Dance Chronicle* version included detailed annotations and a bibliography, which are here omitted. Those wishing to consult them are referred to *Dance Chronicle* volumes 25 nos. 1, 2, & 3, and 26 no. 1.

Grateful thanks to Leslie Getz for making available Serge Leslie's unpublished reminiscences of Cyril Beaumont and the photographs therefrom; also to Jill Anne Bowden for much generous help and advice; to Sarah C. Woodcock who steered the author through the Beaumont Collection in the Theatre Museum, London; to Mollie Webb of the library of the Imperial Society of Teachers of Dancing for assistance on Beaumont's long association with the society and its *Dance Journal*; and to Mary Clarke and the editorial staff of *The Dancing Times*.

In 1931 Serge Leslie, an American dancer in London with a passion for books about dance, found his way to Cyril Beaumont's bookshop. Reminiscing in 1989, he wrote:

I, today, have no clear idea of how I arrived there. Was it up from Trafalgar Square, or down from Cambridge Circus? In any event I suddenly came upon this small shop at 75 Charing Cross Road, with its Harlequin and His Bat sign, and its window full face with a beveled one leading to the doorway; bursting with dance books. I imagine three or four paces would encompass the store front, and yet its windows and doorway were blazing with interest. New York, Chicago nor yet Paris had ever had the display this simple store front offered.

He was captivated, went in, met the quiet man who owned the shop and was taken through to the minute sanctum from which Cyril Beaumont planned and pursued the vast network of worldwide activity that was to make him one of the most influential non-dancing personalities ever associated with theatre dance.

At the time of Leslie's visit Beaumont was forty, halfway through his remarkably diversified career. He had owned and run the Charing Cross Road bookshop, bought for him by his father, since 1910, when he was nineteen. It fulfilled a boyhood fascination with literature and rare books that resulted in a firm ambition to be a bookseller. With the shop had come a remarkable assistant, Alice Beha, his elder by some years, enthusiastic and knowledgeable. He wrote of her in *Bookseller at the Ballet*:

A tall, well-proportioned young woman, some five foot six in height, with beautiful arms, a silky skin, and a clear complexion. Her features, inclined to be round, were dominated by an aquiline nose and a brow high and broad, which conferred upon her a benign air. Her eyes were brown, her hair was dark brown and built up on the top of her head, a style known as Pompadour… In the shop she generally wore a blouse and ankle-length skirt over which she tied a black apron.

Alice introduced him to ballet. The year before, she had been greatly impressed by Tamara Karsavina, who had danced at the Coliseum with a small group that included Theodore and Alexis Koslov and Alexandra Baldina. Initially Cyril resisted this enthusiasm. Apart from plays, which were at that time his main theatrical interest, he had seen ballets only at the Empire Theatre, where (in spite of Lydia Kyasht, their current *première danseuse*) he had been more intrigued by watching the ladies of the town who dominated the promenade. So it was not until April 1911 that he took Alice to the Palace Theatre to see Anna Pavlova and her partner Mikhail Mordkin. To his surprise, he was greatly stirred: 'Until then I had no conception that dancing could rise to such heights. The dancers and the music were one, and they seemed able to express every emotion they pleased.'

Absorbed by this experience, Cyril did not catch up with the Diaghilev Ballet until the following year. He heard accounts of the sensational first London season in June 1911, and writes, 'I was minded to go, but I felt that nothing could surpass Pavlova and Mordkin, and I stayed away.' He decided differently in 1912, when he was brought the exquisitely produced souvenir book of Diaghilev's season in Paris. The splendid reproductions of Bakst designs and the fine photographs of Tamara Karsavina and Vaslav

Nijinsky beckoned him toward the theatre. So, on 18 June 1912, he and Alice went to Covent Garden to see a performance.

Cyril was immediately enthralled. This is something about which he has written in great and fascinating detail in *The Diaghilev Ballet in London*. What has nevertheless to be added is the changing context in which he continued to watch the Diaghilev Ballet. On that first occasion, when he saw *Thamar*, *Les Sylphides* and the London premiere of *L'Oiseau de feu*, he was only twenty – younger than the principal dancers – slight, fine-boned, auburn-haired, confident because of an enlightened and supportive family background and excellent schooling, and master of his thriving little bookshop. Among his many talents he had an innate ability to observe, remember and record details of performances. As a writer he had already contributed articles to a short-lived literary periodical, *The Interlude*, and was training himself to think analytically and critically.

He has left us a vivid record of Adolph Bolm in *Thamar*:

> You must imagine him as a dominating personality with a big head, swarthy face, high and prominent cheek-bones, large mouth, determined nose and dark piercing eyes. He had a strange head, half warrior, half musician, the embodiment of action and intelligence.

That night Karsavina delighted him with her contrasts. She danced in all three works. In *Les Sylphides*,

> she was poles apart from the Karsavina of *Thamar*. The vampire Queen had become a tender wraith with beautiful regular features and the dark brown liquid eyes of a gazelle … All her movements were soft, rounded and infinitely graceful. There was nothing forced, nothing affected… Her timing was admirable, she knew to a second how long to hold a pose.

As the Firebird, wearing the original costume of orange gauze trousers, a greenish bodice trimmed with feathers, and a feathered cap, she was the embodiment of 'a captured bird passionately longing for freedom'.

The sensation of the evening, however, was Nijinsky:

> His features were inclined to be Mongolian with their high cheekbones and the curiously slanting eyes… he had unusually muscular thighs and his calves were overdeveloped, even bulbous. But his every movement was so graceful that he seemed ideal, almost godlike… While dancing *terre à terre* he seemed never to touch the ground but always to travel just above it. His elevation was prodigious. There was no flurry, no seeming preparation; he vaulted upwards, or bounded forwards, with the effortless ease of a bird taking flight.

Much developed from this first encounter. Cyril's commitment to the company's performances became total. During the seasons before World War I started in August 1914, he completely familiarised himself with the repertoire and the artists involved. He became a subscriber, booking front amphitheatre stalls at five shillings a time (prices then ran from two shillings in the gallery to five guineas for a Grand Tier box). No one with a knowledge of ballet history is unaware of the impact of the Diaghilev productions, choreographically, musically and visually. It was very much a Michel (the French form was usually used then) Fokine repertoire, and his works ranged from *Les Sylphides* to *Petrouchka*. Scores by Stravinsky for *L'Oiseau de feu* and *Petrouchka* were new and exciting. Designs by Léon Bakst and Alexandre Benois were breathtaking in colour and style.

The relationship between Cyril and the Diaghilev Ballet was not the largely passive one that most ballet-lovers have with companies of their choice. It began, indeed (as it has for most of us), with regular watching and with audience friendships struck up during intervals. Cyril recorded one of these that he made, around 1913, with a Belgian, Gustave de Beer, who knew Serge Diaghilev and several of the dancers. De Beer was the first to point out Diaghilev to Cyril:

> I saw the profile of an impressive figure in full evening dress, greeting friends and acquaintances, moving with slow stately tread down the gangway of the orchestra stalls... He had plump rounded features, black hair with a white streak about the middle of the forehead, and rather full lips shaded with a neat silky moustache.

Cyril and Alice were now engaged to be married, and de Beer would go back to the shop with Cyril after performances, armed with a very special Viennese gateau, to drink hot chocolate with her. The basement, entered by a spiral staircase, had four rooms; at that time one of these was furnished as a sitting room complete with piano, where Cyril and Gustave analysed the ballets and played melodies from the scores on the piano. The ballet people also began to come to the shop, to browse or sometimes to buy, but also to discuss all manner of things with this acute, totally interested young man.

Another contact took Cyril to Paris. Although his mother's family were not French, they had lived extensively in France and he had grown up bilingual. In fact, people who knew him well (such as the sisters Nancy and Jill Anne Bowden) feel that he was possibly more relaxed and easy over speaking in French than he was in English. Before the first Diaghilev Ballet season in London, he had been in touch with Maurice de Brunoff, editor of *Comoedia Illustré*, about souvenir programmes, and in 1912 went across the Channel to discuss the 1913 Special Number of *Comoedia Illustré*. At the same time he contacted François

Bernouard, director of La Belle Édition, who had published George Barbier's *Vingt Dessins sur Vaslav Nijinsky*. Another call was to a shop kept by Paul Iribe, where he saw the magnificent photographs of Nijinsky taken by the Baron de Meyer.

Nijinsky himself came into Cyril's shop. He looked around, he said nothing, he bought nothing, he went away. Bolm also came, and occasionally took Cyril out to lunch to talk about his own ambitions for the future. A call from an artist called Robert Montenegro proved fruitful. He had made a set of drawings of Nijinsky in black and white touched with gold, and Cyril decided to publish them as a portfolio with a preface that he himself wrote. In the preface, Cyril stressed the contrast between the vigour and virility of Bolm's stage presence and the otherworldliness of Nijinsky's art:

> His characters are never those of a human being; they are all products of fairy stories, ancient folk lore or mythological legends… He does not seek to depict the actions and gestures of an isolated type of the character he assumes; rather does he portray the spirit or essence of all the types of that character.

Cyril continued to make friendships with fellow Diaghilev Ballet enthusiasts, as well as with book buyers and collectors. There was the American poet John Gould Fletcher. Letters he wrote from Paris kept Cyril in touch with seasons there. There were Osbert and Sacheverell Sitwell, who first came to the shop in 1913 while they were still at Eton. They and Cyril had a raft of interests in common – not only ballet, but also other forms of theatre, including *commedia dell'arte*, military history (Cyril had a lifelong dedication to Napoleon and Wellington), painting and poetry. Through Osbert he met the painters Paul Nash and Walter Sickert, and later the young composer William Walton.

Another fellow ballet-lover was Adrian Allinson, a painter, stage designer and musician, who collected piano scores of Russian ballets. From him Cyril bought his first picture, a painting of the Vauxhall Gardens scene in an Alhambra Ballet production.

The year 1914 began with a balletic disturbance: Nijinsky formed an independent company with his sister, Bronislava Nijinska, which appeared at the Palace Theatre in early March. It was not a success. Staging problems led to audience discontent and managerial quarrels; the small repertoire included a version of *Les Sylphides* that differed choreographically and musically from Fokine's; and Nijinsky himself lost magic away from the Diaghilev Ballet context. The season was cut short when he became seriously ill.

The Diaghilev Ballet, without Nijinsky, was at Drury Lane from 20 May. Fokine himself danced as Daphnis in his own *Daphnis and Chloe* and as the Golden Slave in *Schéhérazade*. The season included the first Fokine staging of *Le Coq d'or*, which was simultaneously sung and danced by two sets of performers. Karsavina was the Queen of Shemakhan, and Cyril writes of how she conveyed that

> her smiling enigmatic face... with its hint of the exquisite delights in her gift, was a mask for a sinister purpose... those sinuous arms with their languorous movements could strangle as well as caress... From the moment (she) made her appearance, her beautiful but mocking features dominated the piece, reducing the brilliant figures around her to the level of marionettes which she controlled with the skill of a puppet-master.

At the end of the season came a significant debut, that of Léonide Massine in *La Légende de Joseph*. As Cyril describes him:

He appeared little more than a boy, well formed, handsome, with curly black hair, swarthy features and dark lustrous eyes. [He] showed himself worthy of the confidence which Diaghilev had reposed in him, for the young artist's performance had a dignity and poetry that have not faded from my recollection.

During that season Cyril decided to write a book about Karsavina. They met for the first time at the Savoy Hotel. The meeting went well – she provided him with a curriculum vitae handwritten on hotel notepaper and a Russian brochure of tributes paid to her. Later she accepted an invitation to tea in the shop basement. Nothing came of Cyril's plan because of the outbreak of war, but much later, in 1922, he published in translation a study of her work by Valerian Svetlov.

By now Cyril was a seasoned book dealer, buyer and seller. Although his literary interests remained wide, he was also, inevitably, specialising in publications relating to dance and ballet. In March 1914 John Gould Fletcher decided to go home to America, and asked Cyril if he would care to buy his library. Cyril managed to raise the money, and in May his twenty-first catalogue included the Edition de Luxe of Arsène Alexandre's *Decorative Art of Léon Bakst* and Ludwig Kainer's *Ballet Russe*, a collection of fourteen lithographs of its dancers. His twenty-second catalogue was issued in June/July; he records that it was

> printed in sanguine, the cover being a reproduction of a charming engraving of amorini from *Caprice d'un Bibliophile*. The items offered numbered 475, and included original lithographs by Charles Conder, sketch books associated with Mrs Gaskell and Charlotte Brontë, George Moore's very rare *Flowers of Passion* and *Confessions of a Young Man*, and etchings and etched frontispieces by Félicien Rops. At the same time

we issued a separate eight-page catalogue: Books and Illustrations of the Russian Ballet. Nowhere else in London was there such a selection on offer.

Beaumont was never a conceited or self-promoting man. This simple statement of excellence is merely a matter of setting down an accurate fact, something about which he was always deeply concerned. At this point, when World War I was imminent and he was about to marry Alice after their eight-month engagement, it is appropriate to fill in some facts about his family and early life. As he chronicled this himself in remarkable detail, I shall limit myself to matters that I feel are of special importance to an understanding of the man, his life and his work.

Cyril William Beaumont was born in Lambeth, London, on 1 November 1891. Both father and mother had fascinating backgrounds. His father, Frederick, grew up as the son of a Yorkshireman who toured the country with his World of Magic show of stage illusions, which included mesmerism and phrenological readings. Frederick had none of his father's flamboyance, but inherited his passion for electricity and mechanics. Cyril describes him as a generous and caring man, but with no sense of humour and a tendency to violent tempers. He became a teacher of electrical and mechanical engineering, a physicist, an experimenter in natural philosophy, and an inventor, 'a man who lived with machines and was always thinking of them'. Cyril's mother, Mary Balchin, was the daughter of William Balchin, a top-class jockey and later racehorse trainer and breeder, who was employed in Holland, in England (by the Duke of Hamilton) and later in France at Chantilly (by the Baron de Rothschild).

Cyril grew up in North London. He had a sister, Vivien, and a younger brother, Bryan. As a small boy he had extra tutoring in

English and French grammar, theoretical chemistry and mechanics. He had piano lessons, and went to France and Belgium with his father; sadly, his mother was greatly limited in her activities, as she had lost her eyesight through a brain tumour. He played eagerly with a large collection of toy soldiers and he discovered puppets and toy theatres. At twelve he went to the Stationers' Company School. He read avidly, studied chemistry and formed a Scientific Society with some schoolmates. Such multiple interests and pursuits almost inevitably led him to fail his matriculation examination twice, and at that point, much against his father's will, he declared that he would like to become a bookseller.

World War I started on 4 August 1914. Cyril and Alice were married on 10 December and took a flat in Rosebery Avenue. In 1915 Frederick Beaumont died. Cyril tried to enlist in the army but was turned down because of a serious knee injury, so he went on building up his bookselling business and extending it into antiquarian fields. Rare books on ballet and dance were always featured in his catalogues, but in no way exclusively, and the catalogues themselves were presented with great care. A remarkably wide subject range of books, manuscripts and other items was offered for sale by this young man. Selecting at random from catalogues produced during the war years, one finds a signed first edition of *The Picture of Dorian Gray*; Thomas Davis's *Memoirs of the Life of David Garrick, Esq.*, with 104 engravings of actors and actresses; *Les Poésies de Stéphane Mallarmé*, with an etching by Félicien Rops; a first edition of Thomas Hardy's *Wessex Poems*; rare editions of Conrad, Yeats, Shakespeare and Marlowe; and prints by eminent Japanese artists. Reading the lists makes it apparent that Cyril was already regularly in touch with most people of note in his world of book dealing.

Cyril and Alice Beaumont at a garden party in 1929.

Cyril's artistic association with an outstanding illustrator, Vera Willoughby, began in 1915. At that time she contributed cover designs for four of his catalogues, Nos. 24, 28, 29 and 30. In a study of her work in the journal *Ibis*, William Connelly describes the first of these, Spring 1915, as being a version of a watercolour painting, *The Lesbian Flute Player*, which Cyril bought and owned until his death. He sold another of her watercolours, of Karsavina and Nijinsky in *Le Spectre de la rose*, to the collector Pickford Waller for the sum of three guineas – and claimed that he had often lamented that sale: 'The painting captured admirably the lilt of Weber's music with the dreaming girl and the Spirit of the Rose wreathed about by drifting petals.' Her cover for catalogue 28, in 1916, was of 'a stalwart Bacchante, braced to dance, one hand brandishing a thyrsis and the other shaking a tambourine'.

By 1917 Cyril felt sufficiently established to launch his own publishing imprint, the Beaumont Press. From then on there were two distinct highways in his life. In Katherine Adelman's interesting master's thesis, *The Critical Writing of Cyril W. Beaumont*, in which she analyses with great diligence his style and approach as a ballet critic, she describes him as 'the first Englishman in the 20th century to make a career of studying and writing on dance', but his primary career was as a bookseller and publisher. Studying and writing on dance did not pay his bills, nor was it his sole interest, even though it was of immense importance both to him and to the dance world.

The intention of the Beaumont Press was to fill a publishing gap by producing fine limited editions of contemporary authors and poets. Cyril's aim was to choose unpublished work and present it in unique volumes with selected paper, bindings and decorations. He wrote in *The First Score*, 'Being deeply interested in the literature of our time, it seemed to me a pity that modern writers should not be afforded an opportunity of having their works published in a choice form during their lifetime.' This policy was carried through in twenty-six books over the years from 1917 to 1931. Cyril designed each one, commissioning artists to contribute appropriate illustrations; after the first three volumes he printed them himself on an old Albion hand press that he introduced to the shop's basement.

The first of this exquisite and exclusive list appeared on 1 September 1917. Its full technical details (and those of all the other volumes) can be found in an article by Barry T. Jackson in *The Private Library* of Spring 1975. Cyril had decided to begin with contemporary poetry, and asked John Drinkwater 'to contribute a collection of poems which would make about forty pages'. It was titled *Tides*. Three months later it was followed by *The Sunken Garden and other Poems* by Walter de la Mare, for which Cyril provided a cover design by A.J.Vaughan of such a garden 'with a repeated diaper pattern of fruit, flowers, birds and sundials surrounded by a border of trees and butterflies'. Each subsequent volume of the twenty-six was as, or even more, meticulously and perceptively planned.

In 1918 the poets represented were W.H. Davies (*Raptures*), Robert Nichols (*The Budded Branch*) and Drinkwater (*Loyalties*). The following year started with a one-act play by Joseph Conrad (*One Day More*) and continued with poems by Richard Aldington (*Images of War*), D.H. Lawrence (*Bay*) and Herbert Read (*Eclogues*). Aldington had written to Cyril from the trenches on the Western Front, offering his poems. There were considerable postal problems with Lawrence's book, as Lawrence was moving about in Italy and involved in postal and railway strikes. W.W. Gibson (*Home* – the last of the series to be printed by hand in the basement of No. 75) and Robert Nichols (*The Smile of the Sphinx*) were the 1920 poets. The year 1921 began with a difference, a volume titled *After Reading* [Reading gaol]: *Letters of Oscar Wilde to Robert Ross*, and then featured *Crossings*, a fairy play by de la Mare. In 1922 there appeared *After Berneval* (more letters from Wilde to Ross) and a translation of Goldoni's *The Good-Humoured Ladies*. Cyril had greatly enjoyed Massine's ballet and found in the British Museum Library a copy of the play as originally published. Aldington, who was an Italian scholar, translated the work and Ethelbert White provided the decorations, which were planned by Cyril to link the ballet with paintings of the period by Guardi and Longhi; there were also various technical innovations that led to its later inclusion in a British Museum exhibition of fine printing.

In 1923 came poems by Edmund Blunden (*To Nature*) and *The Café Royal and other Essays* by Arthur Symons. Newly discovered poems by John Clare (*Madrigals & Chronicles*), edited by Blunden, was the only 1924 book; Cyril's increasing workload meant that something had to be cut. More poems by Blunden himself (*Masks of Time*) came in 1925, while two books were published in 1926: *Parisian Nights* (essays) by Symons and *The Letters of J.E. Flecker to Frank Savery*. In 1928 there were further Blunden poems (*Japanese Garland*) and in 1929 a memoir, *The Wet Flanders Plain*, by Henry Williamson, while 1930 again featured Blunden's poetry (*A Summer's Fancy*). The last Beaumont Press volume was Blunden's *To Themis*, published on 24 November 1931. It is a prestigious and tantalisingly varied catalogue, and each (now highly priced) book is individually a treasure. An essential part of these books, and of many other of Cyril's publications, was their covers, illustrations and decorations.

Engrossed as he was in the book and publishing side of his life, Cyril did not forget ballet. Early in the war he pursued another idea and made it work. He admired the satirical woodcarvings Caran d'Ache had made of French politicians and decided that this craft could be adapted to create two-dimensional figures of Diaghilev dancers. He collaborated on this with Adrian Allinson. They discussed making ten-inch-high figures out of two-ply wood, cut out with a fretsaw and mounted on detachable stands. They would be in costume, hand-coloured, and in typical poses from various ballets, with the cutting-out done by a specialist firm. Allinson designed nineteen figures, including Pavlova, Karsavina, Nijinsky and Bolm. Fifty copies of each were made, and sold at 7s. 6d each. A complete set of the figures is a treasure of the Theatre Museum in London.

London in those days, just before and during the war, could be described as a network of artists. Everyone working in the performing and visual arts either knew everyone else or at least were related to each other by way of mutual friends. Cyril's acquaintances were drawn from literature, music, and the performing and visual arts. One led to another – as the Sitwells had led to Nash and Sickert – and at one dinner party Cyril met an interesting freestyle dancer and teacher, Margaret Morris, an artist whom he felt to be in advance of her time. Her work had been influenced by Isadora Duncan's brother Raymond and his enthusiasm for Revived Greek Dance, and she had started a studio in Chelsea in 1910, evolving her own method of contemporary dance. She arranged dances, designed costumes, and put on performances with her students in her own small club theatre.

Although there were no exciting foreign visitors in wartime, dancers were a major part in popular West End musicals and revues and in music-hall programmes, often in choreography by Edouard Espinosa. The ballets at the Empire Theatre that Cyril had failed to enjoy continued, now mostly starring a fine English ballerina, Phyllis Bedells. Adeline Genée gave farewell performances in 1917, and away from the Empire a delightful young leading dancer emerged in Ninette de Valois, who developed from a child star in 1914 to be *première danseuse* at Covent Garden during the 1919 (Victory) opera season. That year she also took a small group, led by her and the Russian Serge Morosoff, on a music-hall tour.

Cyril had kept in touch to some extent, by way of reports and correspondence, with the vicissitudes of the Diaghilev Ballet, and in the summer of 1918 a man attached to the company in an undefined business capacity called in to see him. Zenon (he seems to have been generally known only by that name) reported that in spite of wartime difficulties Diaghilev was negotiating with the theatre manager, Sir Oswald Stoll, for a London season. Delays ensued, but the company opened at the Coliseum as part of the music-hall bill on 5 September.

It had of course changed in personnel and even in repertoire in its years of absence. One significant difference was that the boy Massine was now a principal dancer and choreographer, and the excitement on the first evening was his ballet The *Good-Humoured Ladies*, in which Lydia Lopokova was an unforgettable Mariuccia. Cyril wrote that

> her personality was a complete surprise to me. She remains the only dancer I have ever seen who was a born comedienne. Petite and well formed, she was as lively as a London sparrow. She danced not only with her limbs, but with her head, her eyes, her shoulders and even her lips.

With the new dancers and some new designs, changes of emphasis appeared in the well-loved former repertoire. Cyril has pinpointed them in his writings. In *Cléopâtre*, Lubov Tchernicheva was 'cold, enigmatic, sadistic… quite different from the voluptuous woman presented by [Serafina] Astafieva'. In *Carnaval*, the role of Pierrot 'had shed something of the dramatic importance associated with Bolm's interpretation'. The ballet now 'took on the air of an innocent romp at a children's party, whereas previously on the surface, all was gaiety; but, beneath the maskings and dalliance, you were conscious of a certain mockery and cynicism, even a hint of tragedy'.

Cyril soon met Lopokova when her Italian husband of the time, Randolfo Barocchi, came into the shop looking for a book and introduced himself. A valuable friendship was established, and through this Cyril became more a part of the company than at any time previously. Always, however, he sustained his natural role as an observer, a recorder and an increasingly experienced critic. As the six-month season progressed, more Massine ballets were shown – *Midnight Sun* and *Children's Tales* (*Contes Russes*) – and other dancers made their mark: tiny, mercurial Stanislas Idzikowsky, Leon Woizikowsky and an English ballerina, Lydia

Sokolova. Cyril continued to estimate and analyse; soon he would write it all down.

Never content without some new project, Cyril now planned a series of small books on Diaghilev ballets. The format was to be enlarged and used to great effect many years later with *The Ballet called Giselle* and *The Ballet called Swan Lake*. Each was to have an account of the ballet's origins, theme, music and designs, and also to deal with the action of the ballet and the way important roles were performed. In his own words, 'I wished the description to capture something of the dancers' actions and movements.' Initially he did not intend to do the writing himself, but when he tried to recruit another writer he was not happy with the result. The monographs, under the collective title *Impressions of the Russian Ballet*, were therefore his first excursions as a writer about dance.

Four books launched the series: *Cléopâtre*, *The Good-Humoured Ladies*, *Carnaval* and *Schéhérazade* (all probably chosen for the topicality of the 1918/19 Diaghilev season). Instead of photographs, line drawings by Adrian Allinson were used, hand-coloured by either Cyril or Alice. Every detail was lovingly decided. For *Cléopâtre*, the cover design copied the pattern for her scarf; for *Good-Humoured Ladies*, 'a dancer was seen against a view of Venice, printed in Venetian red on a warm brown paper'; for *Carnaval*, its backcloth blue was used with a dado of black and gold; for *Schéhérazade*, a Moghul hunting scene was printed in blue on yellow. Later books in the series were *Petrouchka*, *La Boutique fantasque*, *L'Oiseau de feu*, *Children's Tales*, *The Three-Cornered Hat*, *Thamar* and *The Sleeping Princess Parts I and II* (in 1921). Two other books Cyril published that year were linked with Russian ballet. One was an English version of *The Tale of Igor*, with illustrations by Michel Sevier; the other a translation of Pushkin's *The Golden Cockerel*. The series of wood figurines was continued, with more attention to detail, using artists other than Allinson – Randolph Schwabe, Michel Sevier, Ethelbert White and Vera Willoughby.

The first year of peace, 1919, saw the Diaghilev Ballet at the Alhambra Theatre from April to July. New ballets included *The Three-Cornered Hat* and *La Boutique fantasque*. Massine's star was in the ascendant. Cyril's friendship with Lopokova and Barocchi flourished in regular meetings when they 'would discuss the inexhaustible subject of Ballet', a phrase that everyone enamoured of the art must find familiar. He also had, from Diaghilev, a pass to watch every performance and take along an artist to make sketches. He was allowed to go through the pass door during intervals and either watch the stage being set or sit in the greenroom, where Diaghilev would be discussing productions with artists like Picasso or Derain and Laura Knight was sketching dancers. Such privileges could turn a head less totally balanced than Cyril's. As it was, he remained true to his innate character, absorbing every experience with relish and constantly working on new personal notions.

The only sadness came after the splendid launching of *La Boutique fantasque*. The marriage of Lopokova and Barocchi was in trouble. Barocchi was driving her to overwork and she was exhausted, so on 10 July she simply did not turn up at the theatre. Vera Nemchinova took over as the Can–Can Dancer. Karsavina had returned, and it was she who created the Miller's Wife in *The Three-Cornered Hat*. After July there was a short lull in Russian ballet activity, but at the end of September the company gave a season at the Empire Theatre. Lopokova was still absent, but Cyril had a contact in Idzikowsky, whom he had known for some years. Sitting in his dressing room and seeing him make up for character roles was a fresh interest. Cyril commented that, 'Few things are more fascinating to watch than the widening of an eye, or the thinning or broadening of a nose, by the adroit disposition of certain lines of colour.'

Apart from the Russian Ballet there were home-grown stirrings of some significance in 1919, and Cyril was not unaware of them. Bedells had left the Empire and was freelancing. At Covent Garden she appeared with Alexander Gavrilov in Granville Bantock's *Pierrot of the Minute*. Then, for Lahda, a newly formed Russian society directed by Theodore Komisarjevsky, she danced with Laurent Novikov in a one-act play, *A Merry Death*, and two ballets, *A Fisherman's Love* and *The Prince and the Groom*. In November the local dance world staged the first of a series of important Sunshine Matinees. These were founded by Mrs Dorothy Claremont, the organiser of a charity called Sunshine Homes for Blind Babies, in conjunction with the founder-editor of *The Dancing Times*, Philip J.S. Richardson. The matinees were held annually until 1930, and the programmes brought together the best of the British dance world together with interesting overseas artists. Thus, in 1919 the bill included Karsavina, Astafieva, Bedells, de Valois and Carlotta Mossetti, who danced at the Empire Theatre. Margaret Morris and her student Kathleen Dillon also appeared, and another eminent Revived Greek Dance teacher, Ruby Ginner.

In 1920 there was only one Diaghilev Ballet season, at Covent Garden in June, when Massine's *Pulcinella* was staged and Cyril became intrigued by the history and background of *commedia dell'arte*. At the end of the season Massine left the company. Meanwhile, Cyril was engaged in another project. In 1918 he had been taken by Lopokova to see Maestro Enrico Cecchetti teach, and he gradually began to feel it was vital that there should be some record of Cecchetti's method of training. Cyril knew that as a non-dancer he was not fully equipped to undertake such a task. He arranged for Idzikowsky to demonstrate the positions and exercises used in Cecchetti's classes so that he could write them down. This practice worked well until Idzikowsky went abroad with Diaghilev. Cyril explained the situation to Cecchetti, however, and together they settled into a different pattern. They embarked on daily discussions: Cyril spent the days at his shop and then met Cecchetti about 6 p.m.; they worked until ten or eleven and next morning Cyril would go over his notes, type them out, and have them ready for checking that evening. They spoke mostly in French, as Cecchetti's English was limited. As an additional check, Cyril tested his notes with a pupil of Cecchetti's, Nellie Ferguson. The collaboration was remarkably smooth. Cyril describes Cecchetti as

> inclined to embonpoint, but very quick and active in movement. He was just under medium height. He had a fine large head, his grey hair close-cropped at the sides, but somewhat bald on the crown. His plump, clean-shaven features were the colour of ivory, relieved by a faint ruddiness at the cheekbones. His eyes were blue grey, very bright and alert… and they sparkled with a benign air, or a whimsical note of mockery, according to his mood.

The book needed illustrations and Cyril chose Randolph Schwabe, at one time head of the Slade School, to do the diagrams, based on positions demonstrated by the maestro himself but representing an ideal imaginary male dancer. Lopokova demonstrated *pointe* steps and Cyril posed for head movements. Schwabe also made a magnificent lithograph portrait of Cecchetti, which hangs in the library of the Imperial Society of Teachers of Dancing (ISTD), and contributed distinguished illustrations to a great many books published by Cyril. The preparation of the Cecchetti book took some months and it was only in 1922 that *A Manual of the Theory and Practice of*

Classical Theatrical Dancing (Méthode Cecchetti) finally appeared.

During the Manual's preparation, Cecchetti's wife, Giuseppina, was very much a part of the undertaking. When he wrote an obituary of her in *The Dance Journal*, Cyril commented warmly about how she would take over class for her husband if he were tired out or unwell, and would then 'just as easily relinquish the cane for the frying-pan'. He remembers the pleasant hours in Wardour Street and how she 'played mother' to all dancers, whether from the Diaghilev Ballet or students of the school. She provided 'coffee or chianti, as age befitted', and was 'endowed with that rare sympathy by which she could cry or laugh with one, accordingly as one felt sad or happy'. He remembered also her delicious miniature performances as the Marquise in *The Good-Humoured Ladies* or the Russian wife in *La Boutique fantasque*, and was sad to think he would not see them again. He continued, in words with which all lovers of ballet can empathise:

> Year by year we see our favourites in their famous parts and so we come to regard them as permanent as a painting, a piece of sculpture, or a book. Death grows envious and before even such a possibility has entered our minds the dancer is no more. The once bright picture fades more or less quickly into a vague mist, and with the passing of time only a little trick of tilting the head or a familiar gesture of the hand remains imprinted on the memory.

In 1920 there were other highlights. In March at the Coliseum there was a notable production of J.M. Barrie's one-act play *The Truth About the Russian Dancers*, which starred Karsavina (in a mime role) and a small ensemble of dancers. In April, Pavlova returned to Drury Lane for an 8-week season. She was partnered by Alexander Volinine, and the programmes included

Amarilla, *Chopiniana* and *Flora's Awakening*, as well as *The Dying Swan* and, in its London premiere, her solo *The Dragonfly*. In December there was a short season at the Palace Theatre by the avant-garde Ballets Suédois, directed by Jean Borlin. Also in December the Association of Operatic Dancing of Great Britain (now the Royal Academy of Dance) was launched. Cyril has left no record of these happenings, but it is improbable that he did not go to most of them. In fact, a photograph of Pavlova chosen by him for inclusion in *Bookseller at the Ballet* shows her as the Dragonfly.

However, he was always committed to the Diaghilev Ballet, and it had a season at the Prince's Theatre (now the Shaftesbury) on 26 May 1921. Massine was absent and Woizikowsky inherited most of his roles. To Cyril's delight, Lopokova returned. A suite of Andalusian dances, *Cuadro Flamenco*, was performed by a group of Spanish gypsy dancers and guitarists – a form of theatre presentation with which we have become extremely familiar, but which was novel to London audiences of that time. Cyril was captivated, and in later years wrote much about great Spanish dancers. He thought that the leading woman, Maria Dalbaicin,

> was one of the most beautiful women I have ever seen. She had a fine figure, regular features of classic beauty, and a complexion smooth as marble, bronzed by the sun and set off by a wealth of dark silky hair which gleamed like old lacquer. But with all her beauty there was something strangely sexless about her… she danced with a pure, if cold, classic grace.

About this time, Cyril followed up *The Art of Lydia Lopokova*, which he had planned and published in 1920, with *The Art of Lubov Tchernicheva* (1921). The Lopokova album contained portraits of her by Picasso and Glyn Philpot. For the second album Cyril commissioned Philpot to paint a frontispiece portrait of Tchernicheva, and Vera Willoughby (credited as Vera Petrovna) to contribute hand-coloured drawings of important roles in eight ballets: *Cléopâtre*, *Carnaval*, *The Good-Humoured Ladies*, *L'Oiseau de feu*, *Schéhérazade*, *Children's Tales*, *La Boutique fantasque* and *Les Sylphides*. Willoughby studied Tchernicheva in performance, and Cyril was delighted by

> the accuracy with which she had caught the dancer's features and physique, and the details of her costumes. [Willoughby] possessed the magical quality of being able to invest a character with a sensuousness which created the illusion of having in depth an eye, a mouth, lips: even a finger could invite a caress and whisper of a profane love.

Other dance features in 1921 included a small Danish group from the Royal Theatre, Copenhagen, led by Elna Jorgen-Jensen and John Andersen, who danced excerpts from *La Sylphide* and *La Ventana*, which might have been Cyril's first taste of Bournonville. Karsavina and Novikov appeared in another J.M. Barrie play, *Pantaloon*. At the Kingsway Theatre, a brave shot at a British Ballet was organised by Marian Knight, including *Les Petits Riens* ('reconstructed from the indications left by J.G. Noverre, its original inventor'), an original ballet *The Snow Queen*, and a *Harlequinade with Dialogue*, something Cyril would surely not have missed, as he was increasingly intrigued by Harlequin's history.

Nothing in 1921, however, measured up to the enthralling spectacle of the Diaghilev Ballet production of *The Sleeping Princess* at the Alhambra on 2 November. Cyril was part of this epoch-making event from the beginning, attending rehearsals as well as performances, and he has described it in vivid terms. There is no need for me to add to his descriptions, but one remark establishes the context in which he was watching and writing:

The theatre became a kind of ballet club, for night after night you would see the familiar faces of certain enthusiasts come to relive the ballet and enjoy its enchanting melodies and compelling rhythms, music that dancers could feel with all their bodies and which inspired them to exert their talents to the utmost. This interest was stimulated by changes in the cast so far as the two principal roles were concerned.

More than twenty years later this could have been written about the long season of *The Sleeping Beauty* with which Sadler's Wells Ballet reopened Covent Garden in 1946.

Throughout his life Cyril was always thoughtful about gifts and good wishes for his dancing friends. In the Theatre Museum, London, there are letters he kept from a great number of well-known dancers, frequently thanking him for flowers or telegrams marking first performances, personal events, or illness and accidents. This winter of 1921 he mentions how he personalised presents. For Lopokova there was 'a little work-box in the form of the crown she wore as the Lilac Fairy'; for Nemchinova 'a treasury-note case of vellum tooled with a carnation in pink and gold' – she danced the Carnation Fairy. For Cecchetti, who gave one performance of Carabosse, a role he had created thirty-two years before, there was a vellum scroll with portraits of him in famous roles, and a short tribute.

After the commercial failure of *The Sleeping Princess*, the next Russian Ballet season in London, in April 1922, was by a group of dancers led by Massine, Lopokova, Woizikowsky, Sokolova and de Valois at Covent Garden in a mixed ballet divertissement and film programme. Similar engagements followed at the Coliseum. As a publisher, Cyril brought out an album of ten photographs of Lopokova, with a portrait of her as Columbine by Randolph Schwabe, and an Edition de Luxe of Valerian Svetlov's study of Karsavina. This book was translated by Helen de Vere Beauclerk and a Russian friend, Nadia Evreinov; decorations were by Lovat Fraser, and illustrations by Allinson, Schwabe, Natalia Gontcharova, John Singer Sargent and others.

In December a major project of Cyril's, the Cecchetti Society, was launched at a dinner at the Astoria Hotel. The intention of the Society was to propagate and explain the Cecchetti Method, and the founding committee, apart from Cyril, was made up of Margaret Craske, Friderica Derra de Moroda, Ninette de Valois, Jane Forestier, Molly Lake and Marie Rambert, with Cecchetti and Mme Cecchetti as president and vice-president. Cecchetti, unwell, returned to Italy in 1923, and de Valois resigned. In a letter to Cyril she wrote that 'there are so many points on which my views differ from those of yours and the other members of the Society that I feel my presence on the Committee is a stumbling block to its success rather than a help'. In the course of time, however, she and Cyril became firm friends.

In 1924 the Cecchetti Society amalgamated with the ISTD as a self-contained part of the Faculty of Cultural Dancing. Formed in 1904, predating by 16 years the Association of Operatic Dancing of Great Britain, the ISTD's application was very much wider than operatic dancing; it was a society for teachers of every kind of dance throughout the British Empire. From its headquarters in London it held examinations and issued its own diplomas. Cyril was particularly appreciative of its scope and variety, and in 1924, while remaining chairman of the Cecchetti Society, he gladly became a member of the ISTD Administrative Council, wryly noting, 'I did not then foresee that I should serve in that position for nearly fifty years and in the course of time become first Vice-Chairman and finally Chairman [of the ISTD].' At all these stages he identified closely with every branch of the Society's activities. From 1950 he offered an annual prize for a Cecchetti Society choreographic competition, and in 1958 arranged a performance of winners' works. In gratitude for all he had done, in 1952 the Society founded a Cyril Beaumont Scholarship, which contributed to the fees of a 2-year course for a Cecchetti student at the Royal Ballet School.

Starting in 1921 Cyril wrote articles on dance in a journal called *The Dancing World*, a now obscure publication. The first number of the journal was dedicated to Leslie Henson, 'the inimitable comedian', who wrote: 'The title is an inspiration – for what a Utopia it suggests – our war-scarred planet dancing the past into oblivion.' That number was still primarily slanted to ballroom dancing, apart from a little verse about Pavlova:

Pavlova charmed us at the Lane
And likewise at the Coliseum.
We've gone again and yet again
And sung our secular Te Deum
To one before whose grace there twirled
The incense of a nation's homage.
Who better rule The Dancing World
(The answer's Who?) from youth and from age.

No later issues are in the British Library archives, but one or two reviews were included in Cyril's 1949 book *Dancers under my Lens*. It sounds as if they had a long way to go before they could raise the literary standard enough to lure Cyril into print, but when he did begin writing about what was going on in the theatre, his attention extended beyond classical ballet into all forms of dance. For example, in May 1922 at the Coliseum, Ruth St Denis returned to London after a long absence. Cyril made several pertinent points, starting with the fact that 'it is due mainly to her influence that Western peoples have learned to appreciate the truth and beauty of Oriental dances... she took the basic elements of several and arranged them in such a manner that they would be readily intelligible to a Western audience.' He found her a great artist:

> Her art is imbued with the Eastern tradition which ordains that all expression shall be centred in the body, hands and arms; and not in the legs and feet after the Western ideal... Her hands can be sharp and angular as though hewn out of stone, they can curve and writhe like a flexible strip of steel and yet sway as delicately as a leafy branch breathed upon by a light spring breeze... She has achieved that summit of Oriental art by which after a series of coordinated gestures, a new unexpected movement is made, and the pose retained for a brief interval.

In praising St Denis he took the opportunity to censure any (unnamed) lady 'who thinks that all that is necessary is to wave her bare arms and legs to something of Chopin, Grieg or Mendelssohn' and call it classical dancing. By this he meant non-balletic, freestyle dancing based on ancient Greek influences.

In July, Cyril saw another important non-ballet dancer, the Canadian Maud Allan, at the Winter Gardens in Bournemouth. He sketched her career: how she had started as a pianist, turned to dance, and given her first performance in Vienna in 1903 and her London debut six years later. After describing the stage setting – a simple dark-green velvet curtain – he went on to praise her dancing:

She moved with a light tripping movement or else walked quietly *sur les demi-pointes*. She was the incarnation of some nymph from a mythological forest, some naiad of the sea… Her musical training had served her well, for each movement was a true, harmonious and exact expression of the music that evoked it.

However, he was not happy about the composition of her dances:

Her vocabulary of gesture is limited in the extreme… when each musical phrase of identical construction was interpreted in the same manner ad infinitum, pleasure faded to weariness… [She] is undoubtedly a lady of high artistic intelligence with a delicate musical sense, but the ineffaceable bane of her art is repetition.

He went on to discuss the difference between classical dancing and academic ballet. Academic ballet had 'a vast selection of steps, an infinite number of permutations', whereas in classical dancing the dancer had to found 'a whole new grammar of mime and movement', which, obviously, he felt had not yet happened.

In 1923 Lopokova and her group were still appearing at the Coliseum, Pavlova and Novikov had a September season at Covent Garden, and the Sunshine Matinees continued, with guest appearances by Camille Bos and Gustave Ricaux from the Paris Opéra Ballet. In September, Fokine came to London to choreograph the dances in a spectacular production of James Elroy Flecker's play *Hassan*, for which Delius composed incidental music. Cyril arranged a series of meetings with Fokine, intending to produce a book about him. An unexpected point arose when Cyril gave him samples of the descriptive accounts of his ballets; Fokine liked them, but 'thought them almost too realistic and consequently far too helpful to anyone wishing to reproduce his work!' He did, however, talk about his methods of composition and rehearsal techniques. Again, Cyril leaves us with a keenly observed description of the man:

> [Fokine] was under middle height and slightly built. He was dark, clean-shaven, growing bald, with a small straight nose, small eyes, small mouth, and a somewhat quizzical expression. He was quiet and reserved in manner, but radiated an unmistakable authority. He could be devastating in comment and on occasion display a pawky humour which was biting.

In December 1923 for *The Dancing World* Cyril wrote about the husband-and-wife team The Sakharoffs, who had appeared in October at the Adelphi Theatre. The Russian Alexandre Sakharoff, a solo recitalist, had married a German dancer, Clotilde von Derp, and they toured extensively with an idiosyncratic style of modern dance and mime. Cyril described them as lithe and supple, with extraordinarily expressive hands and arms, but a very limited repertoire of steps. He wrote of Clotilde as 'a most engaging person whose movements and personality radiate an unusual freshness and gaiety. She is like a spring breeze which wafts to the nostrils the odour of tender shoots and budding flowers.' Alexandre was totally different: 'He is neither Greek god nor savage warrior, but a strange, subtle creature – part exotic, part fantastic, part sinister, part macabre, reminiscent of the bizarre creations of artists like Bayros, Beardsley or Rops.'

He found that they understood 'the meaning of style, of grace and of beauty; their ideas are of a refreshing originality, and they have every right to be termed artists'. He also felt that they were 'well worthy of the study of every dancer', and, in fact, even Massine was greatly influenced by them.

Cyril's dance horizons were constantly being enlarged. In

1924 the British Empire Exhibition opened at Wembley, and for an article commissioned by the quarterly *Opera* he went to see a troupe of Burmese dancers and musicians. Once again, we are now familiar with the form of presentation, the on-stage musicians with strange musical instruments and a dance style involving a wide range of unfamiliar movements, all of which were novel in the 1920s. Cyril was charmed with the flexible, almost boneless, effect of the trained hands, the fluent arms and expressive head movements, and the subtle footwork. He also saw Tibetan male dancers with wonderful human and animal masks performing dragon and peacock dances.

An ongoing enthusiasm with Cyril was the character of Harlequin. After first acquaintance with this magical immortal through pantomime harlequinades, his interest continued with Fokine's *Carnaval* and increased after Diaghilev staged Massine's *Pulcinella* in 1920. This was based on a *commedia dell'arte* scenario found in a manuscript book in Naples, and it led Cyril to a study of *commedia* masks and characters. He traced Harlequin from the sixteenth century onwards, writing some articles about him in *The Dancing Times* that were expanded into a book, *The History of Harlequin*.

The History of Harlequin demonstrated the thorough way in which Cyril approached theatre research. Book after half-forgotten book, from the seventeenth and eighteenth centuries to the late nineteenth century, were almost casually mentioned to support the fascinating subject of the development (and decline) of the *commedia dell'arte*. Theories that the Arlecchino of Italian comedy is a direct descendant from ancient Roman mimes were discussed (and to his belief dismissed) by reference to works such as Maurice Sand's *Masques et Bouffons* of 1860 or *Memoirs of Carlo Gozzi* as edited by John Addington Symonds in 1890. Details of costuming and of plays and their performance in

France and England as well as in Italy were meticulously examined.

In 1924 Cyril also translated and published an English version of *The Birth, Life and Death of Scaramouche*, written in French in 1695 by Angelo Constantini, which dealt with the most famous early interpreter of Scaramouche, an Italian comedian named Tiberio Florilli. Cyril attempted to relate the English text to the French stylistically by studying English seventeenth-century writers (how could this man do so much, while still continuing his bookselling and publishing career!), but he recruited Edmund Blunden to transpose a few verses into English rhymes.

There were other balletic events in 1924. In January the Coliseum engaged Boris Romanov's Russian Romantic Theatre Ballet for a season, which Cyril covered for *The Dancing World*. It was a large group, led by Elena Smirnova, Elsa Kruger, Claudia Pavlova, Romanov and Anatole Obukhov. Their repertoire included a version of Petipa's *Les Millions d'Harlequin* called *Harlequinade*, which Cyril greatly disliked:

> If M. Romanov's presentation was a faithful copy, I can only say it was a great pity that he dragged it from its deserved oblivion… The theme was feeble, completely unconvincing, and most of the dances were very dull… If there is a particular inferno to which wicked artist-dancers are consigned, I cannot conceive a more exquisite torture than their being forced to witness an eternal performance of *Harlequinade*.

The second week's programme, however, was a great improvement. It contained a pantomime-ballet called *Andalusiana*, with music by Bizet and choreography by Romanov. A highly histrionic piece about love affairs and rivalries in a Spanish tavern, it included a lengthy knife-duel. Cyril thought it was danced and mimed extremely well, and summed up by saying that 'the ballet is not blatant melodrama, it is very carefully staged, and the dances and fight are calculated to thrill the most blasé balletgoer'.

There was always plenty to see at the Coliseum. After the Romanov company came Lopokova and Idzikowsky in divertissements, while Idzikowsky and Vera Savina led a Massine ballet, *Les Roses*, which had been premiered in June at the Soirées de Paris. Mordkin turned up in October, with Julie Bekefi and Lydia Semenova from Moscow. With hindsight, of course, the most important event, also in October, was the appearance in a variety programme at the Empire Theatre of four unknown Russian State Dancers, whom Cyril lists as he then knew them: Tamara Sheversheyeva (later Gevergeyeva or Geva), Alexandra Danilova, George Balanchivadze (soon to become Balanchine) and Nicholas Efimov. Cyril was particularly impressed by Danilova, 'a slim, vivacious, dark-haired young woman with laughing eyes', who danced with Balanchivadze and Efimov in a *pas de trois*, *Matelotte*.

The Diaghilev Ballet returned to the Coliseum on 24 November with Bronislava Nijinska as choreographer, Nemchinova the leading ballerina and Anton Dolin the *premier danseur classique*. Other famous names were Tchernicheva, Sokolova and Woizikowsky. De Valois, who had joined the company in 1923, was programmed as Nina Devalois, and cast lists also include Alice Nikitina, Felia Dubrovska and Anatole Vilzak. Soon Diaghilev also engaged the four Russian State Dancers, and Balanchivadze was turned into Balanchine. It was a short season but the company was engaged to return in May 1925.

Cyril was introduced to Nijinska's work by *Le Train bleu*,

inspired by sports such as tennis, golf and swimming, which gave Dolin his big chance in an athletic leading role. He also met Diaghilev's new young secretary, Boris Kochno, who was increasingly influencing artistic decisions. When Diaghilev introduced Cyril to the latest promising discovery, Serge Lifar, he saw

> a handsome young man, with dark hair, dark lustrous eyes, and an engaging smile; his skin was burned by the sun to an attractive shade of brown which suggested a creature of the woodlands. I thought to myself that if only he had pointed ears, he would resemble one of those fauns which figure so frequently in 18th century paintings of mythological subjects.

He adds, drily, 'In later years the part of the Faun in Nijinsky's ballet was one of Lifar's favourite roles – indeed there were occasions when he even performed it solo, excluding the nymphs.'

During 1924 Cyril had talked over with Philip Richardson of *The Dancing Times* the idea of translating J.G. Noverre's *Lettres sur la Danse et sur les Ballets*. He also wanted, on the technical side, to work as far backwards from his Cecchetti Manual as possible; other titles in view would be Thoinot Arbeau's *Orchésographie* (1588) and Rameau's *Maître à danser* (1725). Richardson shared this interest in historic books, and was already building up a remarkable collection – a collection that was much in the news at the end of the twentieth century when the Royal Academy of Dance, to whom he bequeathed it, put it in the hands of a dealer for sale. Both men wished to make available to English students key books on dance from the past. Cyril started with Arbeau, for the music enlisting the help of the young composer Philip Heseltine (aka Peter Warlock), who had specialised in Tudor and pre-Tudor

ORCHESOGRAPHY

A TREATISE IN THE FORM OF A DIALOGUE

Whereby all manner of persons may easily acquire and practice the honourable exercise of dancing

BY

THOINOT ARBEAU

Now first translated from the original edition published at Langres, 1588

BY

CYRIL W. BEAUMONT

With a Preface

BY

PETER WARLOCK

Published by C. W. Beaumont, Printer and Bookseller, at Number Seventy-five Charing Cross Road, London
MDCCCCXXV

The title page of Cyril's translation of Arbeau's Orchésographie.

music; *Orchesography* in Cyril's translation was published in 1925. In 1926 Warlock wrote *Capriol Suite*, based on tunes from Arbeau's manual, which Frederick Ashton was to choreograph in 1930 for the Rambert Dancers.

Cyril took on a new responsibility in December 1924: to edit, and contribute to, *The Dance Journal*, the organ of the ISTD. Editing the bimonthly *Journal* was demanding work – nothing Cyril ever undertook was a sinecure. It offered detailed teaching descriptions of dances and examination syllabi as well as a variety of articles. Typically, he applied himself to every aspect of the Society's affairs. His first article, in December 1924, pulled no punches at all. Under the title 'The British Dancer, some Criticisms and Suggestions', he summed up the contemporary scene without any rose-coloured spectacles, deploring the fact that dancers in Britain lacked the kind of Ballets Russes company that would provide an orchestra directed by a first-rate conductor, music from famous composers, and high-quality settings and costumes. Most of them also lacked 'the power to excite emotion… and a sense of style-atmosphere'.

Over the next few years *The Dance Journal* included a stimulating coverage of historical and topical matters. Cyril used it unashamedly to serialise research matter on which he was working about Rameau, Marie Taglioni, Fanny Elssler, Auguste Vestris, Jules Perrot and the history of ballet in Russia from 1613. Most of this was later cannibalised into book publications. He included, however, a splendid range of other subjects by specialists. There were articles by F.M. Kelly on historic costume; by Harcourt Algeranoff on Japanese dance; by Friderica Derra de Moroda on works by Heinrich Kröller (*Skyscrapers*) and Gunter Hess (the first *Façade*); by Hedley Briggs on the making of masks; by Melusine Wood on period movement, Irene Mawer on the art of mime, Alice Chamier on the pyrrhic dance, and

Ragini Devi on classical Indian dance; and by himself on the history of choreography or dance notation. He wrote substantial book reviews of publications such as *My Life* by Isadora Duncan, *Theatre Street* by Karsavina, *Divertissement* by Dolin and *Nijinsky* by Romola Nijinsky. There was a series by Derra de Moroda of interviews with choreographers, 'How I Arrange My Ballets', that included Balanchine, Massine, Bolm and de Valois. Cyril himself occasionally reviewed dance events or wrote on talking points such as the teaching of dance history, or applause and the dancer.

In 'On the Teaching of Dance History', he stressed the vital point that

> progress depends on the cultivation of the student's interest… The history of dancing is bound up with court ceremonies, changes in social conditions, the development of costume, the history of the theatre, the story of nations and many other matters; and it is only by showing dancing in relation to them that the lesson can be made really interesting.

In the piece about applause he wrote, 'Applause is a quality vital to the success of a representation.' Legitimate applause, he considered, was gained for only four reasons: skill, personal charm, the ability to please and the power to simulate and transfer an emotion. Reprehensible conduct was responding to applause 'in an affected, careless or unbecoming way'. He condemned, of course, the paid claque, but observed that 'this curse is almost non-existent in the British theatre'. The article may have prompted the dancer Harold Turner to write to him, saying, 'I will think seriously on the manner of taking one's calls, it is so important.' Turner had already been singled out by Cyril in a short piece in the *Journal* in June 1930. He was a Cecchetti student and Cyril analysed his progress, assessing him very accurately for his technical ability: good balance and elevation, excellent pirouettes and batterie, and pleasing *port de bras*. 'He has the youthfulness and high spirits of a larking schoolboy... but he needs to beware against a tendency to allow this gaiety to run away with him... he is persevering, hard-working, and full of promise; he is certainly a dancer on the horizon.'

New developments characterised the two seasons of the Diaghilev Ballet at the Coliseum beginning 18 May and 26 October 1926. In May there was the London premiere of Nijinska's satirical and stylish *Les Biches* (translated as *The House Party*). According to Cyril,

> It was not a pleasant theme and it was presented with an insight that could only be derived from an intimate knowledge of such occasions, but it was a genuine portrait of a phase of contemporary life, a presentation all the more piquant by the very delicacy of its imputations.

Sokolova was the Hostess, Nemchinova the enigmatic Girl in Blue. Cyril was intrigued by choreographic innovations in the latter role: 'The shoulders were square to the audience... and in certain gliding movements were dipped and raised in a wave-like rhythm, while the arms, either bent at the elbow or extended in the same plane, were disposed in angular positions, following the same line.'

Other novelties followed, such as Dolin dancing *sur les pointes* in Nijinska's *Les Fâcheux*. There were new scores by Poulenc (*Les Biches*) and Auric (*Les Fâcheux* and Massine's *Les Matelots*), and designs by Marie Laurencin (*Les Biches*), Braque (*Les Fâcheux*) and Pedro Pruna (*Les Matelots*). In October, Massine choreographed *Zéphyr et Flore* to music by Dukelsky and designs by Braque, in which Lifar had his first important role, as Zephyr's brother. Balanchine created his first ballet for the company, *Barabau*, to music by Rieti. A displeasing little story about a farmer and some very coarse peasants, it filled Cyril with misgivings as to the wisdom of Diaghilev's choice of Balanchine as choreographer.

De Valois had left Diaghilev, and she opened a school, the Academy of Choregraphic Art, in London in March 1926. Cyril was briefly in touch with her because he had an ambitious plan to form a small company of young British dancers. He needed a collaborator who would choreograph dances or miniature ballets, for which he had several ideas, and act as teacher and ballet-mistress. One of his ideas, never to be realised, was for a Fire Dance, about 'the birth and death of a fire, performed by dancers in draperies of grey, yellow and red, with headdresses shaped like tongues of flame. I sketched a scenic panel on the shapes of leaping flames, and Allinson designed the costumes.' He discussed the idea of a company with de Valois, but found that she was too preoccupied with her burgeoning career as a teacher, dancer and choreographer.

His second choice was Margaret Craske and he got farther with her. They decided to call it the Beaucraske Company and planned a small repertoire. Cyril designed a setting of adaptable basic architectural features (arches, columns, a balustrade) made in light wood. They would be painted grey and coloured by lighting. He was sufficiently avant-garde to envisage projecting painted slides on the grey surfaces. Craske arranged the dances to Cyril's suggestions (although he did a little choreography himself) and rehearsed pupils from her classes. The repertoire included a burlesque ballet, *Circus*, with a succession of 'turns', with designs by Wyndham Payne and music composed by Fred Adlington; a *Tumblers' Dance* (based on a medieval painting); *Bullfight*, with a picador riding a basket hobbyhorse; and an item called *Temples d'amour*, set to Chabrier music, with couples seen in silhouette, flirting, embracing and quarrelling. Unfortunately, no bookings were found, so the Beaucraske Company ended.

Cyril, however, revived the idea with Flora Fairbairn, a well-known teacher. She already had a performing group called the Mayfair Dancers, but they set up a new venture called the Cremorne Company and this time it reached the stage for a couple of performances. The dancers included Penelope Spencer, Stanley Judson, Frederick Ashton, and Audrey Ashby, who had danced with Romanov's Russian Romantic Theatre Ballet as *première danseuse*. They made their debut at the Scala Theatre on 11 March 1926, with a repertoire that now included *The Christmas Tree*. Cyril wrote the scenario, based on Hans Andersen's *The Little Match Girl* but set in a London square in 1840. As the young girl, sitting in the cold outside a wealthy house, lit her matches to warm her hands, she fancied that the Christmas-tree toys she saw through the window danced for her: the fairy doll, the humming top, a nut pursued by a frightening pair of nutcrackers, and a sprig of holly competing with a sprig of mistletoe to gain the attention of a Christmas cracker. It ended happily when two young men took the match girl inside the house, where she was welcomed to the festive fireside. Music was again by Adlington and designs by Wyndham Payne – Cyril kept not only these designs, but also a set of cut-outs Payne made of twelve of the characters, mounted on small metal bases.

Ashton made his stage debut in this ballet as a Cruel Old Man, and was also a sword-waving dervish in an enlarged version of *Circus*. Cyril already knew him. He had come into the shop to ask advice about a teacher and Cyril had sent him to Massine, who, when he left England, recommended Ashton to Rambert. In 1926 Ashton was on the threshold of his future fame – in June the Marie Rambert Dancers appeared in the revue *Riverside Nights* at the Lyric Theatre Hammersmith, and Ashton choreographed his first ballet, *The Tragedy of Fashion*. The Cremorne Ballet's programme also included *Bal Mabille*, based on Paris night life in the 1890s; *Primavera*, a solo suggested by Botticelli's painting, set to music by Daquin; and a *Buffoon Dance*, based on illustrations in Lambranzi's *New and Curious School of Theatrical Dancing*. Never staged was an idea for a French Revolution ballet to be called *1789* – a pity, as Cyril had commissioned music from Felix White and persuaded Nijinska to choreograph various *pas de deux* for Louis XVI and Marie Antoinette. There was to be no future for the Cremorne Ballet, but some items were included in divertissement programmes given by Fairbairn's Mayfair Dancers at the Royal Academy of Music. Cyril himself appeared there as the Ringmaster in *Circus* and the Lady Killer in *Bal Mabille*, and a little later on he composed a solo for Audrey Ashby, *Lady into Cat*.

In June the Diaghilev Ballet was at His Majesty's Theatre with Nijinska's monumental *Les Noces*. Cyril saw it from the wings, where he could watch the conductor, Eugene Goossens, coping with the percussion ensemble, four pianists, four solo singers and chorus. Although the ballet 'surprised and puzzled both audience and critics' and 'was regarded as a curiosity rather than the work of art it really was', Cyril was greatly impressed by it:

> Nijinska had succeeded in conveying a deeply felt idea: the solemnity of the marriage rite among peasant folk and the spiritual and enduring quality of a mutual love with its exchange of vows meant to be kept. The ballet was a rare and moving experience for those members of the audience prepared to share a mood of reverence.

Other new productions were less satisfying:

The company had shed something of the Russian soul, which was the source of its strength. Many of the new works were slick and slight; whipped-up soufflés instead of meat and wine… one found a suggestion of Riviera spa: brittle, chic and with, despite its elegance, a thinness of spirit.

Sacheverell Sitwell was enlisted by Diaghilev to advise on an English ballet, and various musical and design sources were mooted. One combination that Sitwell suggested, designs based on Rowlandson and music by Boyce, emerged, interestingly, many years later in de Valois's *The Prospect Before Us* (1940). The connection must be Constant Lambert, who may well have given Sitwell the idea in 1926, and in 1940 was musical director of Sadler's Wells Ballet. Diaghilev's English ballet ended up as *The Triumph of Neptune*, with a score by Lord Berners and designs based on Pollock Toy Theatres. Choreography was by Balanchine, and the premiere was on 3 December 1926. Cyril obviously enjoyed many of its pantomime elements, but it was not destined to last. In fact, the Diaghilev Ballet had only one London season in 1927, in June, which included the modernist works *La Chatte* (Balanchine) and *Le Pas d'acier* (Massine). Both had slight themes but novel choreographic and design ideas. In *La Chatte* Cyril liked the athletic-gymnastic use of well-trained and well-formed young bodies; in *Le Pas d'acier* he was pleased with Massine's 'masterly impression of the rhythmic power and beauty of machines'. He was far less happy with Massine over *Mercure*, which seemed to him to be 'stupid, vulgar and pointless'.

In 1928 the Diaghilev Ballet staged Balanchine's *Apollon Musagète*, which Cyril greatly admired, and Massine contributed *Ode*, about which Cyril wrote, 'This ballet, certainly the most extraordinary of a host of unusual works, was a philosophical treatise expressed in terms of light, line and movement.' Its designs by Tchelitchev were far ahead of their time in their use of unexpected materials, of a line of variously sized crinolined marionettes manipulated by the dancers, and of multiplying mirrors. The choreography was equally inventive, and Cyril was wholeheartedly enthusiastic:

> It is not easy to convey the strange character, the celestial beauty, and the intellectual appeal of *Ode*. Those extraordinary designs suggested... animations of the diagrams illustrating Euclid's propositions; and yet always in and out of those corded mazes, moved, crouched, leaped and glided those beautiful unknown forms.

On the publishing side two books absorbed his attention at this time. One was a book of drawings by Eileen Mayo, of Lifar in his best-known roles, with a foreword by Boris Kochno. The other, funded by the ISTD, was an edited English edition of Lambranzi's 1716 *Neue und Curieuse Theatralische Tantz-Schul*, which Cyril had found in the British Museum Library. This was a book of character dances, partly drawn from *commedia dell'arte* but partly derived from work movements. For example, there were dances based on bootmakers stitching or blacksmiths forging, or on pastimes such as tennis and shooting. Cyril remarks on how difficult it is to accomplish something really new: 'here will be found Nijinsky's tennis ballet *Jeux* anticipated by some two hundred years... and a pose which recalls Nijinska's *Les Noces*'.

Two deaths affected Cyril personally: Cecchetti's in November 1928 and Diaghilev's in August 1929. The last Diaghilev Ballet season had started in June. Massine was gone; Dolin had returned. Balanchine staged *The Prodigal Son* for Lifar and Dubrovska. Cyril was impressed with 'its sombre grandeur' and even more by Lifar:

> Lifar's role in this ballet was mime rather than dancing, and he revealed himself a fine exponent of that difficult art. His actions seemed to come straight from the heart, as though he felt the moving story in every fibre of his being. When the ballet ended, I felt conscious of having witnessed one of those rare performances that constitute a landmark in one's memories, something to be treasured and relived.

Diaghilev's death led to a fruitful diaspora throughout the world of his great choreographers and dancers. It also spurred on ballet developments in Britain. Early in 1930 the Camargo Society was founded – the impetus came from Philip Richardson and the twenty-six-year-old Arnold Haskell – to arrange for regular ballet performances that would unite the various strands of talent existing in the UK. It was to draw on the very young companies of de Valois and Rambert, and also enlist existing principal dancers. Choreographers, musicians, composers and designers contributed to the very varied works produced.

Cyril wrote in *The Dance Journal* about the first Camargo performance, given in October at London's very new Cambridge Theatre. For a number of reasons he was not happy about a revival of the *Ballet of the Nuns* from Meyerbeer's opera *Robert le Diable*, a nineteenth-century piece that had been staged for Adeline Genée at the Empire Theatre in 1909 by her uncle Alexander. The best item was Ashton's *Pomona*, to music by Constant Lambert, 'a sound and well-balanced piece of work'. Ashton was progressing well:

> His groupings showed an increasing sense of design, his movements were more graceful, more rhythmic, and more

closely related to the music; and there were lovely melting dances for Pomona [Anna Ludmilla] and her nymphs, and strong manly dances for Vertumnus [Dolin] and his immortals.

Ludmilla 'looked like a goddess and danced like a goddess', and Cyril was charmed by Dolin, whom he had always regarded as 'a first-rate dancer and nothing more', finding that he displayed 'a graceful bearing and a sense of restraint'. Lopokova spoke, saying that the audience was present at the birth of English ballet. Cyril took issue with this, listing five lines of names of people who had already done much for English ballet. For himself, he welcomed the new Society, but pointed out that this first performance had shown no new dancers, no attempt had been made to give unknown but talented English dancers a chance in solo parts, no definitely English ballet had been staged, and no unknown choreographer had been launched.

At this point, one can begin to see an important divergence between the two historically orientated and influential *éminences grises* of the British ballet scene, Philip Richardson and Cyril Beaumont. Richardson had most of the trump cards in his hand. He was sixteen years Beaumont's senior, and had been editing *The Dancing Times* since 1910. For his magazine he contributed editorial comment under the pen name The Sitter Out. A tall, elegant, forceful and gregarious man, a ballroom dancer of note and the chairman of the Official Board of Ballroom Dancing from 1929, he was also a historian and researcher. Over the years he was revealed as a power in mainstream ballet, operating on countless committees and always closely linked with personalities and projects. By founding the Association of Operatic Dancing of Great Britain (with Edouard Espinosa) and pushing it on to its Royal Charter in 1936 as the Royal Academy of Dancing (later Dance), and by initiating the well-attended Dancers' Circle Dinners for key people, he established supremacy in manipulating the fortunes of British ballet.

Beaumont, basically much more retiring, had none of the extrovert magnetism of Richardson. He had different ambitions. He was intrinsically a man happy to work on his own and pursue his own ideas in his own way. In a very different style, drier and more reticent, he paralleled Richardson's career, writing criticism for *The Dancing World*, editing and writing for *Dance Journal*, and promoting the fortunes of the ISTD as assiduously, if not as noticeably, as Richardson did for the RAD. The two men converged in their passion for history. Richardson wrote about it in *The Dancing Times* and also published other researchers, such as Mark Perugini and Ifan Kyrle Fletcher. Both he and Beaumont had articles from Derra de Moroda and Melusine Wood. They were ploughing the same field and to an increasing extent becoming rivals.

Beaumont, however, had the advantage of being able to publish regularly books he either wrote, translated or edited. He, too, had his friends, and his ability to make and keep them eventually raised him to a comparable, or even greater, place in the affection of the dance world. Some friends were his alone; some, like Lopokova, he shared with Richardson; a vast number of others he achieved over the years, as the quiet force of his steady integrity and innate kindness became ever more apparent.

The second Camargo programme, in January 1931, included Ashton's *Capriol Suite* (from the Rambert repertoire) and a new ballet by de Valois, *Cephalus and Procris*. This was a disappointment: an uninteresting theme, unattractive dances, and no single style retained throughout. On the other hand, the best work was another de Valois ballet in a very different mood, *Rout*, which she had choreographed in 1927 for the Festival Theatre, Cambridge. Cyril found it 'a very clever orchestration of strong movements, based on those of fly-wheels and piston-rods, synchronised with the music [by Bliss], the rhythm being emphasised by the beating of the dancers' feet'. Memorably, that evening included a tribute to Anna Pavlova, who had just died:

> The orchestra played *Le Cygne* and the curtain went up on an empty stage, lit with the familiar blend of blue light and green. The audience rose as one and remained standing until the last note had died away. It was deeply moving.

Cyril must have remembered the revelation he had experienced back in 1911, about which he had written, 'There were times when I could hardly keep still, so passionately stirred was I by the surge and the rhythm of their movements. For hours afterwards the image of Pavlova and Mordkin dominated my thoughts.' For Cyril so much had already resulted from that evening; it is equally amazing to realise how many more achievements would still result between 1931 and his death in 1976.

The third Camargo Society programme came in April 1931. The outstanding production was another de Valois ballet, *La Création du monde*, set to the score Milhaud had composed for the Ballets Suédois in 1923. She decided to cast it as a Negro dance-drama, and Cyril felt that it was a work of importance and originality:

> It was obviously the outcome of considerable thought and a very successful attempt to use the dance as an art-form to convey the impression of a primitive people seeking to express a lofty aim... It is certainly the most intellectual ballet that an English choreographer has produced.

The evening ended with the premiere of Ashton's *Façade*. Cyril enjoyed the Scottish dance, the milkmaid scene with

Lopokova as the milkmaid, and the Polka *sur les pointes* danced with great vivacity by Alicia Markova. The Valse he found pleasing, but with over-elaborated arm movements. Up to this point, the dances had been 'conceived in a spirit of light burlesque, with little satirical touches which accorded exactly with the mood of the music'. After that, Cyril felt that Ashton had gone wrong and strayed into music hall:

> We had a step-dance in the American manner, followed by a Tango Pasodoble in which Mr Ashton, got up like the Can-Can Dancer of *La Boutique fantasque*, exercised his fascinations on a bashful maiden (Mme Lopokova) anxious to see life... This dance passed the limits of burlesque and was, frankly, low comedy.

Cyril also wrote about the July programme, of which the highlight was the premiere of de Valois's 'masque for dancing', *Job*. He agreed with that description:

> *Job* is an essay in dramatic movement rather than an arrangement of traditional steps. The amount of thought and study and rehearsal that went into the making of this production must have been enormous, but the result fully justified the labour. It was not a flawless work, but the conception and realisation as a whole have established a standard which it will not be easy to match, let alone surpass.

He was unstinting in his praise of Dolin as Satan: 'He contrived to surround his movements with a tangible, if invisible, radiance which really did suggest an immortal.'

Among many mistaken ideas and misjudged conclusions that people have had about Cyril Beaumont is that he was primarily a fan of the Diaghilev Ballet. He was, instead, open to and knowledgeable about all kinds of dance and movement theatre from anywhere in time or place. His critical estimates are perceptive, informed and universally fair – even if, to readers of today, they are presented in a now old-fashioned literary style of long sentences, subordinate clauses and explanatory detail.

In post-Diaghilev Britain, as the Camargo Society confirmed, indigenous ballet was steadily developing. Cyril also wrote about Rambert's Ballet Club, which had given a performance in April 1931. He begins by saying, 'Mme Rambert, the leading spirit in this enterprise, evidently shares my view that there is a definite English public for ballet' and goes on to describe the tiny Mercury Theatre and make the point that ballets produced there 'need to be most carefully considered in relation to this stage'. Two of the works he found unsuitable, *Les Sylphides* because it needed ground-room and height, and *L'Après-midi d'un faune* because it needed little depth, but width and height. He was kind but critical to performances. In *Les Sylphides*, Pearl Argyle had refined grace and charm but lacked expression, and tilted her head backwards too much in arabesques; Ashton was inclined to overemphasise the romantic atmosphere. The divertissements produced more satisfaction. Prudence Hyman was sparkling in *Circus Girl*; Walter Gore was praised when he danced a *Mazurka des Hussars* with Rambert herself.

Much more interesting was a Rambert programme in November, with Ashton's *Mercury* and *The Lady of Shalott*, and Antony Tudor's *Cross-garter'd*. *Mercury*, alas, only succeeded in being very dull, but *The Lady of Shalott* was a hundred times better. In spite of some faults it was quite Ashton's best ballet to date, 'brilliantly conceived, admirably produced, exactly suited to the size of the stage'. In it Argyle was ideal: 'not only is she a classic beauty… but her movements radiated grace and style; in the death scene her miming rose to great heights'. *Cross-garter'd* (based on the baiting of Malvolio from *Twelfth Night*) was Tudor's first ballet. Tudor had 'very wisely tried to work out his ideas in his own way', and Cyril was impressed by its sincerity, workmanship and expressive storytelling. The evening ended with an abridged version of *Swan Lake Act II*, in which he praised Markova's exceptional technique and ability, although he felt she must develop expressive power. In 1931 she was still very young.

It was in 1931 that Serge Leslie made his first, momentous visit to Cyril's bookshop. Their lifelong working friendship was based on their mutual passion for book collecting and research. From the beginning they talked of bibliographic matters, with Cyril telling Leslie of the pioneer experience he had gained when working, in 1922, on his small volume *A Bibliography of Dancing*. Leslie, a dancer himself, and his wife Doris Niles, a celebrated recitalist of Spanish dances, spent much time on the Continent, particularly in Paris, and Leslie began to follow out specific research lines there on Cyril's behalf.

At this time two visiting dancers of very diverse abilities were reviewed by Cyril. In June 1931 the magnificent Argentina gave three matinees at the Adelphi Theatre. What interested Cyril about her dances was their difference from the usual conception of Spanish dancing. He called it 'a pure, thrice-distilled essence' that appealed to the mind but not to the heart. She had refined and transformed its racy and earthy characteristics into 'a stylised dance which depends for its appeal solely on the dignity of its poses, the grace of its movements and the beauty of its line'.

The other visitor was Mary Wigman, at the Globe Theatre in May 1932. Cyril was, not unexpectedly, resistant to 'the extravagant eulogies which certain writers have lavished on this dancer'. Her dances were accompanied by piano and percussion instruments:

> the melodic element is mainly dominated by the rhythmic… the result tends to become monotonous… All her work is invested with a certain stark efficiency which suggests some intricate mechanism in motion rather than a human being… While she herself may be dominated by the most sublime thoughts and the most dramatic conceptions, only a tithe of their import is transferred to the audience.

The Camargo Society continued. In November 1931 came Ashton's *A Day in a Southern Port*, to music by Lambert that was a setting for Sacheverell Sitwell's poem, *Rio Grande* (the ballet was later known by that title). Cyril found the score inspiring, but felt that Ashton had reduced the imagery of the poem to 'an orgy of sailors and their doxies, very suitable for the Folies-Bergère but hardly calculated to raise the status of dancers in this country'. In fact, he obviously felt that the Camargo Society programmes were proving a disappointment. The next one, in February 1932, had Ashton's *The Lord of Burleigh*: 'It reminded me of nothing so much as the familiar trick in which a conjurer taps a hole with his wand in a paper-covered tambourine and pulls out yard upon yard of paper ribbon; the dances seemed just as endless.'

In June, the evening had a special point of interest in *Swan Lake Act II* as danced by the great Russian ballerina Olga Spessivtzeva (known as Spessiva). This was 'a treat… it is a long time since London saw any dancing of this quality'. Cyril felt that, although English leading dancers should be encouraged, 'there is a great difference between encouragement and the fulsome flattery that has been ladled out in some quarters... This kind of thing is the greatest obstacle to progress that could be imagined.' This sentence reflects one of the most important of Cyril's critical tenets. Spessiva, however, enchanted him:

> She has made her body into a superb instrument which she plays to perfection... Here is the rare authentic note which, presuming certain essentials, requires anything from fifteen to twenty years' study for its production. I have no space to detail the poetry of her adages, her beautifully turned pirouettes, her clean-cut batterie, her ballon, her poise, her balance, and her wonderful sense of line – each and all under perfect control.

There was only one doubt: her dancing was 'a little cold to the heart. Her personality partakes of the same character; it is almost ghost-like in its elusiveness and intangibility.' All his life, he wanted more than supreme technical excellence. In 1950, reviewing Balanchine's *Ballet Imperial*, he wrote, 'But to me art is not art unless it engenders in the beholder emotion of some sort.'

Pavlova's death in 1931 was remembered when Cyril wrote and published a slim tribute to her in 1932. In fourteen pages of text and seven photographs, it contrived to capture the essence of her genius. It stressed the value of her worldwide tours:

> It is not often realised how barren of worthy models are our far-flung dominions. There, the young student has to rely for inspiration on the rare occasions when a theatrical company arrives which includes some good dancer or dancers; thus Pavlova's visits were golden days to be dreamed of in anticipation and to become ineffaceable memories... to many aspirants for dancing honours she was their model, their inspiration, and their star.

In describing her artistry he conjured her up for those who had never seen her:

> She danced with such abounding vitality, with such ecstasy of the spirit; she surrendered herself so completely to the mood of the dance, that she became a being transformed. She glowed, became almost incandescent, as it were, from the lavish outpouring of her nervous energy and muscular force.

By the end of 1932 the ISTD, which was operating in premises in the Charing Cross Road very near Cyril's shop, had five branches: Operatic Association, Ballroom, Revived Greek Dance, Stage Dance (newly formed) and Classical Ballet (Cecchetti Method); a little later, a Natural Movement branch was added. Round the corner in West Street, Margaret Craske and Mabel Ryan shared a studio, where the weekly timetable included Karsavina teaching mime, Joan Stenning on costumes and decor, Rupert Doone on stage deportment and makeup, Celia Sparger on anatomical studies and Ion Aulay on music. In addition, once every week Cyril taught General History of Ballet, definitely a rarity then in a dance school curriculum.

Beginning in 1922 Cyril had been painstakingly listing all the books on dance in the British Museum Library, for which no comprehensive subject-index existed, and Philip Richardson had published the results serially in *The Dancing Times*. There were more than four hundred works on technique, history and dancers as well as ballet synopses and keys to stenographic charts – nearly two thousand references in all. The publication advertisement pointed out that 'Those unable to consult the British Museum will quite likely find many of the books in the nearest Central Public Library. Apart from this, much useful information may be gained by a mere perusal of the Bibliography.' It added, with a truly Cyrillian mixture of practicality and sly humour, 'The price of the book is one guinea – the cost of a single private lesson. Can you afford to be without this key to knowledge?' Among the recommendations from named people, including Pavlova, Karsavina and Lifar, it is worth quoting Fokine: 'It is written with knowledge, with neatness and impartiality.' It is also interesting to find that the journal *The American Dancer* wrote, 'Often the author has added evaluation and information as to the authoritativeness and reliability of the book in question. The reading of these notes alone constitutes a considerable education in dance literature.' The completed book was published by *The Dancing Times* in July 1929 as *A Bibliography of Dancing*.

In April 1934 *The Dancing Times* reviewed another of Cyril's books, *A Miscellany for Dancers*, 'a collection of passages from various authors, ancient and modern, which affords most interesting glimpses of the lives of famous dancers. One chapter, The Dancer as Letter Writer, quotes some lines of Dauberval, Taglioni and others. Several of these were reproduced in facsimile in *The Dancing Times* a few years ago.' A charming little volume, well worth a facsimile reproduction today, the *Miscellany* includes sections such as A Chapter of Accidents, Anecdotes about Dancers, Fashions and Trademarks, and Exits and Farewells.

By this time, Cyril was also working, quietly but seriously, on his *Complete Book of Ballets: A Guide to the Principal Ballets of the Nineteenth and Twentieth Centuries*, eventually published in 1937. It was a mammoth task, entailing a vast amount of correspondence with specialists in archives and libraries, checking and cross-checking a multitude of facts about first performances, creative artists and background, first casts, descriptions of action and contemporary press coverage, as well as finding appropriate illustrations. As he says in the Preface, it was 'indirectly, an informal history of the ballet of the period… a glimpse of that great panorama of choreographic achievement'.

The book itself lists people he relied on, one of these being Serge Leslie, who has written about his finds in fascinating detail. Armed with a letter to M. Prudhomme, then the director of the Bibliothèque de l'Opéra in Paris, Leslie had settled down to painstaking research on libretti and synopses in the ballet records. Some had been printed and could be bought; others were copied by a penman who was paid three francs an hour. Cyril planned out the work and, for illustrations, directed Leslie's attention to specific items. Cupboards were unlocked, and in them Leslie found a treasure of scenic designs and maquettes as well as illustrations. These were photographed on glass negatives. The Opéra's museum also yielded scores and bound volumes of nineteenth-century Parisian journals and magazines.

The wide scope of the *Complete Book* meant that, although much material was required from Paris, much, too, had to come from other countries, from Russia, Italy, Austria or Hungary; it would take subsequent books to add Denmark and the United States. Material in French Cyril translated himself (but, typically, double-checked with de Vincheles Payen-Payne, a Jerseyman who was principal of Kensington Coaching College). Lopokova, to whom the book was dedicated, and the translator V. Virkov were credited for Russia; for Italy, Dr Walter Toscanini and the translators Gino Gario and Miss C. Allardyce; for Germany, the translators Derra de Moroda and Herr T. Schuler; for Hungary, the translators Dr Sima and A. Schwitzer. The book began in 1789 with Dauberval and ended in 1937 with David Lichine. An example of devoted scholarship came in *Supplement to Complete Book of Ballets* (1942), which had a twelve-page Corrigenda and Addenda to rectify and add to the 1937 *Complete Book*, for which Cyril had been

Cyril as a child (c. 1898) with his terrier dog Jack. In his own words: 'At this period I wore a sailor suit with short stockings and laced boots. In the colder weather I was made to don a black three-cornered hat and a bright green coat with several capes bound with black braid.'

Portrait by L.M. Fisher in the collection of Nancy and Jill Anne Bowden.

awarded the Palmes Académiques (Officier d'Académie) by France.

In the 1930s there was tremendous dance activity in London. Summers were dominated by the exciting Ballets Russes de Monte-Carlo directed by Colonel de Basil. There were Les Ballets 1933 with choreography by Balanchine, Les Ballets Serge Lifar, René Blum's Ballet de Monte-Carlo, the National Ballet of Lithuania, the Woizikowsky Ballet and the Philadelphia Ballet. There were the Ballets Jooss and Uday Shankar. The Vic-Wells Ballet and the Ballet Club (Ballet Rambert) both developed steadily, with a fine selection of works by Ashton, de Valois, Tudor and Andrée Howard. The Markova–Dolin Ballet performed from 1935 to 1937, and Tudor's London Ballet started in 1937.

Various shorter books by Cyril were published while he was working on the *Complete Book*; in the 1930s he was amazingly prolific. In 1930 he collaborated with Margaret Craske on *The Theory and Practice of Allegro in Classical Ballet* and wrote *A History of Ballet in Russia 1513–1881*. Outside ballet, he had amused himself over the years by writing charming books for children. These had begun in 1924 with *The Mysterious Toyshop*, illustrated by his friend Wyndham Payne. They continued their collaboration with *The Strange Adventures of a Toy Soldier* (1926), *The Wonderful Journey* (1927) and *Sea Magic* (1928). In 1930 there was a book of rhymes for children, called *Toys*. In 1931 he wrote the autobiographical *Flashback: Stories of my Youth*, a delightful and relaxed account of boyhood memories, which had a preface by Sacheverell Sitwell and was dedicated to a childhood friend, Edward Frank Escott, 'in memory of days gone by'. He also published a monograph on Fanny Elssler and a *French–English Dictionary of Technical Dance Terms*.

In 1932, apart from *Anna Pavlova*, he translated *The Romantic Ballet as Seen by Theophile Gautier* – a selection from the ballet notices contained in the six-volume edition of Gautier's theatre reviews, *Histoire de l'Art Dramatique en France depuis Vingt-Cinq Ans*, with the addition of some other critical essays. When this was reprinted in 1947, Richardson reviewed it in *The Dancing Times*, saying that he owned the six-volume Gautier edition which, he wrote, 'would be lost to the present generation but for the fact that Beaumont has chosen some two dozen of the more important ballet criticisms, added one or two others, also by Gautier but not in the volumes in question, and made an admirable translation into English'. In 1933 there was *A Short History of Ballet*, a monograph on Diaghilev and *A Primer of Classical Ballet for Children (Cecchetti Method)*. This was followed by a *Second Primer* in 1935 and a *Third* in 1941. In 1934 there were small volumes on *The Monte Carlo Russian Ballet* and *Three French Dancers of the 18th Century*, and a brochure on Cecchetti. In 1935 came *Three French Dancers of the 19th Century*, *Michel Fokine and his Ballets*, *The Vic-Wells Ballet*, and a monograph on Alicia Markova. Most of these broke new ground.

Reviews in *The Dance Journal* continued. In 1933 he covered some Coliseum events and a performance by the Association of Teachers of the Revived Greek Dance at the Rudolf Steiner Hall. At the Coliseum, he saw *The Whitsun King*, by his *Dance Journal* colleague Derra de Moroda. She did little choreography, but was a writer and historian of catholic variety. *The Whitsun King*, based on Hungarian folk customs, was danced by Dolin and Wendy Toye. Cyril was not uncritical; although he found pleasant and well-contrived elements, there were too many exits and entrances and it all needed more vigour and fire. It was followed by Act I of Katti Lanner's *The Debutante*, an Empire Theatre revival sponsored by the Association of Operatic Dancing, 'which left much to be desired... Is there any point in reviving such ballets?...

they not only serve no useful purpose but they tend to destroy a good deal of the legendary glory associated with the old Empire Ballets.' An acknowledgement of the rivalry between the Operatic Association and Cyril's Cecchetti Society appeared in a reference to Harold Turner, who danced the male lead. Based on the endless argument as to what is the correct technique of operatic (ballet) dancing (which the Association claimed to represent), Cyril pointed out that Turner owed most of his training to the Cecchetti method,

> although, the production being given under the auspices of the Association, the contrary might be inferred... Would it not be fairer to those who have passed its examinations, if the Association made use of its own products throughout or, failing that, gave credit where it was due?

At the Rudolf Steiner Hall the best item was a staging of the celebrated mime play *L'Enfant prodigue*, with Ruby Ginner as M. Pierrot and Irene Mawer as his son. Ginner was a pioneer of Revived Greek Dance and Mawer was an acknowledged mime specialist. Cyril wrote that 'the production was excellent and the miming so allied to the music that they were one'. He also saw a minuet and a gavotte, which 'did not please us at all'. He took the opportunity to point out that historical dances are the most difficult of all to do well. They needed years of research and great understanding of style; otherwise they should be left severely alone.

At the end of 1933 the ISTD staged an important lecture-demonstration on classic Japanese dances, given by 'Japan's most celebrated ballet master, Rikuhei Umemoto, and attended by about five hundred people'. Cyril read the translation of the lecture, which dealt with various stages of preparation, steps and gestures, and the uses of the fan. It 'afforded a unique opportunity for gleaning an insight into the true atmosphere, the line and the theme, of the dances of Japan'. The entire text of the lecture, with photographs, was published a month later by the ISTD.

In 1934 Cyril covered the Ballets Jooss's second London season. He strongly advised people to make a determined effort to see at least *The Green Table* and *Impressions of a Big City*. *The Green Table*, which in 1932 had won the first prize of 25,000 francs offered in a choreographic competition organised by Les Archives Internationales de la Danse, was 'a modern Dance of Death, conceived in the mordant humour of a Rops, a Daumier or a Forain'.

> [It is] not a ballet in the strict sense of the word, where the whole action is danced from beginning to end. It is part dance, part dramatic movement, very modern in treatment and presented with a sure feeling for design in the construction of its groups and ground patterns; while the executants play their part with a delicate sense of the harmony of rhythm and movement, and a dramatic intensity in keeping with the tragic theme.

Impressions of a Big City he relates to a feeling of his own, saying,

> Anyone who has stood at the corner of Piccadilly Circus must have received that sensation of watching the turning of an enormous wheel, whose rim is dotted with figures which sweep into view and then pass from sight. This is the impression produced by this scene.

The Seven Heroes was a lively burlesque, but he found *A Ball in Old Vienna* very thin.

At that time Cyril rarely reviewed the Vic-Wells Ballet,

although he saw their programmes; but an exception to this was de Valois's *The Haunted Ballroom*, staged in April 1934, which he described as 'a room out of Poe's House of Usher peopled with Heine's phantoms':

> The music [Geoffrey Toye], if occasionally reminiscent, has the supreme quality of being eminently danceable and well suited to the theme... The scenery and costumes [Motley] are excellent. Miss de Valois's choreography is most interesting and very musical. The patterns are ingeniously contrived, the action is easy to follow and the eerie atmosphere is maintained in all the dances.

There was, however, a stylistic anomaly – the combination of classical ballet and modern German mass movement. He praised the company, ending,

> Robert Helpmann deserves a paragraph to himself for his excellent rendering of the Master of Tregennis; he dominates the ballet throughout. Not only does he dance well, but he has a real dramatic sense and appreciation of character, which he employs to good purpose in this ballet. We shall watch his career with interest, but this young man should go far.

It was Helpmann's first created role with the Vic–Wells Ballet and the beginning, indeed, of a uniquely stellar career.

In March 1935 the ISTD began a series of annual charity matinees at the London Palladium (capacity 2500) that contained work by each of its branches. Derra de Moroda presented Hungarian dances and Elsa Brunelleschi Spanish dance; there was a Revived Greek bacchanal, Scottish dances and a Natural Movement number. Grace Cone arranged a little ballet, *The Princess Dances*, and the Cecchetti Method was represented by Peggy van Praagh, Maude Lloyd, Mary Skeaping and Bessie Forbes-Jones (later Helene Wolska). A ballroom formation foxtrot was a big hit, as were a cabaret duo (Errol Addison and Sylvia), a tap number (Victor Leopold and six girls) and an acrobatic dance (Laurie Devine).

Cyril also saw Agnes de Mille early in 1935. He commented, surprisingly, on her physical resemblance to Lopokova, saying that they might easily pass for sisters. He was impressed by a solo, *Stage-fright*, which included warm-up exercises, rehearsal and panic over forgotten steps, and ended at the moment when the dancer was called on stage: 'both the conception and the realisation were brilliant'. Another excellent dance was *Try-out*, an impression of a music-hall audition. He considered that she had a varied technique suited to her requirements but was not academically distinguished. She was an excellent mime, with a deft sense of humour. The last review, as opposed to articles on various aspects of ballet and dance, that he wrote for the *Dance Journal* was of the National Ballet of Lithuania, when they gave the first performance in Britain of *Raymonda*, with Vera Nemchinova and Anatole Oboukhoff. Cyril considered that 'as a page from the past the ballet was most interesting but, as an entertainment, it left much to be desired, judged by modern standards'.

In 1936, Serge Leslie records, Cyril talked about one of his long-cherished ideas: to set up a museum for his 'treasures' and a small *salle* where he might give lectures. He asked Leslie if he would be curator of such a museum, but this would have meant that Leslie and his wife, Doris Niles, would have had to give up American citizenship. Leslie would also have had to give up his dancing career and curtail his own book collecting. He explained this to Cyril, who took it philosophically and never mentioned it again. Leslie believed that he never proposed it to anyone else.

The *Complete Book of Ballets* was published by Putnam in 1937. That year also saw the first of his books on ballet design, *Design for the Ballet*. It was idiosyncratically reviewed in *The Dancing Times* by Edward Gordon Craig, who had previously greatly liked both *The History of Harlequin* and *A Bibliography of Dancing*. The period covered was 1914–37 and Craig spent many words denigrating all ballet design between those years as derivative; the only exceptions were the Diaghilev Ballet's *Ode* and *La Chatte*. 'The book reveals how clever everyone is: it is a cleverness which, when applied to the stage, bores us all.' He allowed that it was 'a nicely got-up book and the reproductions are excellent' and that Beaumont

> in a brief and readable introduction containing many a historical note of considerable interest comes at last to say that the possibilities of Ballet today are considerable; it is a most adaptable medium… [Noverre had said] that a *maître de ballet* ought to explore everything, to examine all, since everything that exists in the universe can serve him as a model.

Craig very positively disagreed with this view.

Two books were published in 1938: *Puppets and the Puppet Stage* reflected an interest carried on from boyhood and never neglected; *The Romantic Ballet in Lithographs of the Time* was a collaboration with Sacheverell Sitwell and a very handsome volume.

When World War II broke out in September 1939, Leslie and Niles were in Paris, but he and Cyril continued to correspond. Leslie kept Cyril's letters (and appended them to his unpublished memoir, *C. W. Beaumont – a Personal and Professional Friendship*). They are handwritten on paper headed 'C.W. Beaumont, Publisher of Belles Lettres', with a cablegram address:

Beaulivre London. On 13 November 1939 he was writing from a temporary address, Holmwood Hotel in Boscombe (Bournemouth). He had taken Alice away from London, as she was far from well, leaving his old friend William Beaumont Morris, known as Montie, in charge of the shop. He commented,

> This wretched War is making things very bad for business, but I hope that none the less your tours are going well and are everything you wish. I should like to take this opportunity of saying once again how much I appreciate your great kindness in scouring the Musée de l'Opéra and the Bibliothèque Nationale on my behalf.

He wrote again on 21 November, saying that he was anxious to send them a copy of his recently published *Five Centuries of Ballet Design*. The book was to have come out on 14 October, 'but what with doubts and fears, and difficulties in getting material, it did not appear until Nov. 14th. I was very pleased to see it published, I can tell you, as I thought if it does not come out now, goodness knows when it will.' He mentioned that he had been

> preparing a revised and enlarged edition of the Book of Ballets, including the Bournonville section, which owes much to your kind offices. Unfortunately, this has been definitely held up, which has depressed me considerably. Whether nothing will be done with it until the end of the War I do not know. I can only hope for the best, or that the War will soon be over. Since, however, it does not appear to have begun, it is very difficult to foresee the future [this was, of course, the period of the 'phoney' war].

Cyril wrote to Doris on 21 December, saying that he and

Alice had stayed on in Bournemouth to celebrate their Silver Wedding anniversary (on 10 December) and Christmas, but would have to get back to London after that. The war began in earnest in May 1940, with the invasion of Holland and Belgium by Germany and the start of bombing raids on London. Cyril was worried about the Leslies on the Continent. Doris's mother had written to him for news of them, and Cyril describes what happened in a letter to the Leslies dated 1 December 1940.

> [I] got in touch with the Foreign Service Dept of the American Embassy here and, sending them copies of Mrs Niles' communications, asked them if they would communicate with their representatives in Brussels and Paris to see if you could be traced and what had happened to you… All my communications were most courteously acknowledged but the information was nil.

He was annoyed when Mrs Niles got news before he did, and wrote again to the embassy, only to be told that 'they would cable Vichy on my behalf'. He had no further news until five weeks later, when he heard from Mrs Niles that the Leslies were homeward-bound to the USA.

In the same long letter Cyril sketched his present position. His assistant had been called up, so he and Alice had returned to London in February, 'otherwise we should have had to close the shop, which we certainly could not afford to do'. He wrote of London at that time in a way that rings true for many other Londoners:

> We came back just when the raids began. We decided to give up our flat and store our things and live in an hotel for the war period, all things permitting, and so have been staying at the Thackeray Hotel in Great Russell Street, just opposite the British Museum. We have been quite comfortable here, but

had some narrow squeaks. One night we had all the windows blown out, and on another a delayed action bomb fell quite near and we had to get out at 4 a.m. and go to another place a little distance away. This was a very unpleasant walk, going out in the early morning, with the guns crashing, drone of planes overhead, and the glow in the sky of distant fires… We have had some bombs very near the shop; the blast from one which fell during the night shattered our shop window and I had an awful job to get it put right, as builders and carpenters are in great demand these days. Then the same cause cut off our gas supply… However, the window is patched now, and we are trying to settle down as much as we can when the sirens go off every now and then.

Almost as an afterthought, he wrote about two of his books. He had been translating Pierre Tugal's *La Danse* for an English edition and 'had just completed the job when France collapsed… I fear very much all my work is in vain'. But when he was in Bournemouth he had begun writing *The Diaghilev Ballet in London*; 'I am glad to say that I have completed this in spite of Hitler and expect copies daily. One of the first to arrive shall go to you.'

Was it about *The Diaghilev Ballet in London* that Lincoln Kirstein wrote to Cyril in December 1940? Or had Cyril sent him, belatedly, *Five Centuries of Ballet Design*, published on 14 October 1939? Kirstein thanked him for

a beautiful book… I don't understand how, in the midst of war, you could issue such a lovely volume, so perfectly done in every way. It really is the most marvellous testimony to your courage and resourcefulness and to your country. It makes me feel very badly that while we enjoy peace in this country we have so little to prove ourselves worthy of it.

Philip Richardson's review of *The Diaghilev Ballet in London* in *The Dancing Times* was warm and welcoming. He had

> always regarded Mr Beaumont's *Complete Book of Ballets* as his most valuable contribution to the literature of the ballet. This present volume may be described as an exceedingly useful supplement to that book. It gives a wealth of interesting detail which for want of space could not be included in the *Complete Book*, and much other information that would have been out of place in the more formal volume.

All the same, Richardson, who said he had 'particularly vivid recollections of the 1918/19 season', queried Cyril's statement that Alexander Gavrilov danced Pierrot in 1918; he was suffering from an injury and did not dance. Cyril replied by saying that he did indeed dance and that he had programmes to prove it. [To me, with a long experience of inaccurate programmes, that seems no proof at all, but presumably Cyril had actually seen and recognised Gavrilov as well.]

In a March 17, 1941, letter to Doris Niles in America (Serge was ill), on notepaper now headed 'C.W. Beaumont & Co, New and Secondhand Booksellers, Dealers in First Editions of Modern Esteemed Authors, Autograph Letters, MSS, and Original Drawings & Paintings', Cyril referred again to London's war:

> London certainly has some scars, even Cecchetti's old studio in Shaftesbury Avenue was smashed up with blast, but you would be surprised how cheerfully Londoners put up with these unusual and often trying conditions. You see a shop-front blown to smithereens and the stock in a most awful mess but, two or three weeks, the open window-frame is filled in with Bristol board fitted round one or more panes of glass… Some of the shops have humorous notices such as

More open than ever for business or Never mind the blasted windows, come right in! or Bombed out, blasted out, but not sold out!

He thanked Doris for gift parcels, adding that 'if you would like to send us some little thing, a pot of medium shred marmalade would be a real joy, for marmalade is getting quite a rarity, I do not remember when I last tasted any.' Happily, she responded to this; his next letter, 29 July, thanked her for butter and marmalade, tea and guava jelly. The problems of publishing (in this case the *Supplement to the Complete Book*) were mentioned:

You cannot buy any paper without a licence now and when you have that you are entitled to get a specific quantity if the papermakers have the material and labour to produce. Strawboards are also getting scarce and it is quite likely by the end of the year that the exteriors of books will undergo a change, and either be in limp cloth or in wrappers.

He reported on the war in London:

We had some pretty bad raids in May with bombs falling pretty close… [At the shop] we got a certain amount of damage by blast from a bomb which blew out all our windows, blew off two doors in the basement and brought down two ceilings… The floor of the shop was littered with bits of broken glass and it took us two whole days to clear up. Some books were damaged by being thrown from the shelves, others had little daggers of glass driven into their backs. We have now got the place to rights again, but what with the dust caused by the blast, cement left by the plasterers and dust caused by the demolition of buildings near by, I doubt if we shall ever have all the books clean again.

In a short paragraph, he listed ballet activity in London. Ballet was still alive, although the calling-up of male dancers made it difficult for companies to put on ballets with a number of male characters. All the same, the Sadler's Wells Ballet was at the New Theatre, the combined London Ballet and Rambert Ballet was appearing at the little Arts Theatre, and the Ballet Guild was giving shows at the Steinway Hall.

Preservation and conservation of historic material was always a priority with Cyril. He had been extremely interested in the foundation in Paris of the Archives Internationales de la Danse, endowed in 1931 by Rolf de Maré, the founder of Jean Borlin's Ballets Suédois. No doubt the museum project that Cyril had proposed to Serge Leslie was inspired by the existence of this special collection, which had its headquarters and a small theatre/lecture hall in the rue Vital. It survived World War II and was dissolved only in 1950, when the contents were divided between Stockholm and the Musée de l'Opéra in Paris. In London in May 1941 the Ballet Guild had been formed. It was an organisation that ran a small performance company, ballet classes and club events, and it was proposed that it should also build up a library and archives. This was largely the idea of Cyril, Lionel Bradley (a librarian, ballet writer, collector and researcher), and Deryck Lynham, a younger man. Lynham, an Englishman born in France and, like Cyril, bilingual in French and English, also resembled him in his devotion to historic studies. In the 1940s he was preparing a carefully researched history of ballet, *Ballet Then and Now* (1947), as well as a biography of Noverre, *The Chevalier Noverre* (1950), so Cyril and he had much to discuss. All three men were on the Ballet Guild board, along with an eminent barrister, Christmas Humphreys. The archives began modestly but were built up by donations and handed over in 1945 to a trust company as the London Archives of the Dance. A keen teenager, I was co-opted on a voluntary basis as honorary archivist.

The *Supplement to the Complete Book* appeared in 1942, and again Richardson reviewed it. He mentioned that Joan Lawson, who had been in Russia, had provided much Soviet ballet material. He showed no sign of any coolness towards Cyril, saying that the book was 'invaluable as a book of references but also as a means of recalling many happy nights at the ballet, especially if studied whilst a gramophone is playing the music of the ballet we are trying to recall'. The only bone he had to pick was the absence of an index, omitted owing to shortage of paper in favour of corrigenda and addenda to the parent volume, which he felt could have been held over until after the war.

After the *Supplement*, Cyril continued to extend his record of ballets in *Ballets of Today* (1954) and *Ballets Past and Present* (1955). His search for information led him to contact many people for background information. One of these, as he was preparing the entry about Andrée Howard's *La Fête étrange*, was Ronald Crichton, the scenarist. Crichton replied with a long and detailed letter that described how he had read *Le Grand Meaulnes* by Alain-Fournier, had thought that Fauré music would be excellent for a ballet, and later decided that the two could be put together successfully, which he suggested to Tudor. Tudor showed it to the designer Sophie Fedorovitch, and Crichton and Fedorovitch collaborated on a scenario. But after Tudor went to the USA, Howard, who had also crossed the Atlantic, came back and her great friend the Rambert ballerina Maude Lloyd persuaded her to choreograph the ballet, which was produced in May 1940. According to Crichton, she never read *Le Grand Meaulnes*.

Another contact was Agnes de Mille, whom he was to ask in 1950 for an account of the action of her *Fall River Legend*. She wrote to him, about 'the dance between Lizzie and her mother' – 'it is a momentary flash occurring after the murder, in which she reverts to her life with her own mother'. Later, de Mille wrote that the details of the case were 'first suggested to me by Edward Sheldon who begged me to take the material and make it over'.

Cyril and the Leslies continued to correspond. On 27 January 1943, he wrote about

> such a rush at the end of last year, with so much to do and no one to do it, that it was almost impossible to sit down and write. Sometimes we did not leave the shop until 8 or 9 at night, and were too tired to do anything else but doze or fall asleep in a chair.

He commented that 'there is still plenty of interest in books on Ballet but the demand is less for serious studies than for "pickshurs"'. He mentioned that 'for a long time I have toyed with the idea of writing a study of the ballet *Giselle* but the book is still far from being ready. If all goes well, however, it should be ready some time this year.'

There are always happy side-paths to track in Cyril's activities. Olive Ripman wrote a regular article in *The Dancing Times*, and in 1944 she launched a series of twelve competitive essays, based on exam-paper-style questions. The idea appealed to readers, who began sending in entries. Mrs Ripman arranged for a different adjudicator every month, but her first choice was Cyril as the judge for essays on 'What is understood by a Romantic Ballet?' Typically, he spent time and care over the job, and wrote a report that listed some points he felt should have been considered: (1) the introduction of democratic themes (featuring real people and peasants as opposed to classical gods and heroes); (2) the emphasis on local geographical colour, as in highly picturesque ballets such as *Catarina ou La Fille du bandit*; (3) the introduction of the supernatural element. When the series came to an end – the questions were far from easy, leading to discussions on symphonic ballet, the function of critics, the difference between classical and contemporary ballets, and the difference between ballets and divertissement ballets – the final question was, 'Do you think this competition has been in the interest of the Art of the Dance?' Once again, Mrs Ripman asked Cyril to sum up. He felt that the most interesting and useful questions were

> those which could not be looked up, but which required a good deal of individual thought and consideration… the chief value [of the exercise] was to bring home the fact that the art of the dance depends on very much more than merely moving to music or rhythmic accompaniment, and demands a knowledge of many other arts.

On 1 July 1944, Cyril wrote to the Leslies that *The Ballet Called Giselle* was set up and the illustrations complete, but it had to wait until the printers could get down to machining; private work had to take second place to government requests. He had had great trouble getting paper and cloth for binding, and photographic printing paper was rationed. D-Day had come and gone:

> The news of the landing was received calmly because I think we have become a little inured to extremes of good news and bad. The latest good news has been the capture of Cherbourg by your troops – their achievements have aroused great admiration here.

He went on, in typically understated wartime British:

> We have a new source of annoyance in the shape of flying bombs, launched it is said from the Calais area. They are a

kind of pilotless plane with an explosive warhead. They are getting far too frequent. You hear them come chug-chug-chugging, then they stop, glide down and explode… We have had some far too close to be pleasant… added to this we have a siren installed almost outside the shop… so with the 'alert', the noise of the bombs coming over and exploding, then the 'all clear', a sequence which sometimes goes on all night, one gets rather irritable and short-tempered.

Ballet news included the International Ballet's *Coppélia* and a Jooss Ballet programme that included *Pandora*: '[the box's] contents prove to be such horrors as War, disease, air-raids and the like. You can see that an evening at the Jooss Ballet followed by a night of flying bombs is not conducive to high good humour.'

In *The Ballet Called Giselle*, which did appear in 1944, he extended in scope and depth the format he had laid down in the *Impressions of the Russian Ballet* series. Richardson was enthusiastic. He found it a 'very valuable addition to the literature of the ballet' and that there was good reason to be grateful to Cyril for writing it. It included

A short but trenchant chapter about scenery… a very detailed analysis of the eight principal characters, well worth careful study by dancers and spectators… perhaps the most constructive chapter is the exceedingly clear account of the development of the Romantic Ballet.

In March 1945 G.B.L. Wilson reviewed Serge Lifar's book *Giselle, Apothéose du Ballet Romantique* and found that there was 'little in it that is not in Beaumont's book. The English work is far more valuable and is altogether better produced… [The French book,] although an interesting work, is lacking in the constructive criticism and the agreeable speculative and discursive style of Cyril Beaumont.'

Cyril at his desk, a photograph inscribed by him to Serge Leslie.

The Ballet Called Giselle did indeed appeal not only to scholars, but also to dancers. Evidence of this is found among the Beaumont papers in the Theatre Museum, London. For example, after reading his notice of her performance in the title role for Ballet Rambert, Sally Gilmour (for many people one of the select group of great interpreters of Giselle) wrote to him:

> I do want also to thank you more than anything else for your interest and most helpful advice. I wanted so much to ask you before *Giselle* about several things, but didn't dare to, and intend and am determined to put right all the things you have mentioned… I owe any understanding and sympathy I have for the part to your book on *Giselle*.

An undated letter from Anton Dolin said, 'I want to express my deep and sincere thanks to you for your help, advice and affectionate interest and great knowledge you gave to me over my production of *Giselle*.' Violette Verdy wrote of 'the great help you gave me on the occasion of *Giselle*'. Rowena Jackson, who had danced Myrtha, said, 'You were a great help to me, and made the role so much clearer in my mind.' Leslie Edwards was 'very pleased with such an excellent notice from you [about his Hilarion] and appreciate your further criticism, especially your point about showing the sword to Giselle and Albrecht'. Dancers all over the world were indebted to Cyril for help and encouragement. In addition to writing his books, he was unstinting in person with his listening time and gave constructive advice in a way that was never harsh or patronising. Moira Shearer wrote, 'I shall be coming in to see you as soon as possible with several questions about Swanilda, and hundreds about *Swan Lake*. There isn't nearly enough time to study these roles as thoroughly as I would like.' Elaine Fifield wrote:

> Thank you for your comments on my performance of *Casse-*

Noisette. I found them most helpful and a welcome change from some of the personal and unhelpful remarks which have been passed about my dancing by certain critics. Constructive criticism such as yours really gives one something to work upon, and I hope that if I drop into your shop sometime you will be kind enough to give me a few more words of advice.

Often a regular correspondence ensued. Over the years dancers kept in touch, letting him know how their careers were going. For example, his admiration for Nina Verchinina, expressed when she appeared with the de Basil Ballet in works such as *Les Présages*, led her to write to him from New York during 1934 about how she was thinking of setting up a school and beginning to choreograph small ballets, telling him how she was meeting Martha Graham and studying works by her and by Doris Humphrey and Charles Weidman, and thanking him for his interest: '*J'etais si heureuse de lire votre critique sur ma danse, ça me donne encore plus de courage pour mon travail.*' Often he would say appropriate words in appropriate ears to help dance groups making a first visit to London, or recommend some dancer or choreographer to a talent-seeking overseas company. In 1951, after a group of Spanish dancers came to Britain, Dolores de Pedroso wrote from Madrid to thank him 'for all you did to make our visit to London a success… I should like to tell you how precious your friendship is to us.' Teachers of the eminence of Joan Lawson wrote to him: 'I must also express my deep appreciation of all that you have done to help me on my way through the world of dance and ballet. I shall always be in your debt.'

When Cyril wrote to the Leslies on 1 April 1945, he reported that he had been ill in January. About the middle of the month, he had caught a severe bronchial chill and had to lie up for a month, for it seems that I had also been doing too much for too long and so I had to rest as much as possible. I was not allowed to deal with any business, write books or think about new books, and so you can imagine how far behind my correspondence is.

Alice had had to cope with the shop single-handedly. Cyril mentioned that 'the War begins to look a lot better lately and it really seems as though the War in Europe might end in the near future, perhaps even as early as a month or so.' He was right. Germany surrendered to the Allies on 4 May. A letter from Pierre Tugal, who had been fighting with the resistance in France but was now back at the de Maré Archives in Paris, had reported that the collection had not suffered much from the German occupation, as many of the exhibits had been hidden in different parts of the country. So Cyril took this chance of telling Serge about the London Archives of the Dance.

> We shall have to build up friends before we can launch out. Would it be possible, do you think, to give performances in aid of this venture, or do you think that being a non-American organisation it would be difficult to obtain support?… I have no illusions about the difficulty of the task before us, and I am comforted by the thought it is a project which I feel sure will have the blessing and good wishes of you both.

Once the war was over, various new beginnings took place. In 1939 Richard Buckle had taken a gamble on a new ballet magazine. Called simply *Ballet*, it achieved only two numbers, July/August and September/October, neither of which involved Cyril. In September/October there was a small-type sentence on the contents page to the effect that 'BALLET will not appear again until after the War', and this was what happened. In January 1946, when Buckle was released from the Army, it resumed publication in skeletal form, and the March number was entirely devoted to an article by Cyril on the Sadler's Wells Ballet production of *The Sleeping Beauty*, which had reopened Covent Garden on 26 February. Thereafter he contributed reviews regularly, and there was an increasing amount of dance theatre to write about. Roland Petit's Ballets des Champs-Élysées brought London an unforgettable array of small works and fine dancers. One of the best-remembered now is Petit's very first creation, *Les Forains*, about a tiny group of travelling entertainers. Cyril wrote:

> This is a charming ballet which, with the minimum of scenery adroitly lit, makes a deep impression. It is full of atmosphere and admirably succeeds in evoking the life of the strolling player... The choreography is necessarily spectacular in the stage scene, but graced by many witty and emotional touches.

Next was Le Nouveau Ballet de Monte Carlo, directed by Lifar and displaying another talented ensemble that included Yvette Chauviré, Janine Charrat, Renée (not yet Zizi) Jeanmaire, Youly Algaroff and Vladimir Skouratoff. The repertoire included one four-act work by Lifar, *Chota Roustaveli*, based on the poet Roustaveli's writings, with music by

Honegger, Tcherepnine and Harsanyi, and featured innovative sections of percussion rhythms. Cyril found that the dances tended to be far too long, but he was impressed by the use of Georgian national dance elements and a stirring and ingenious choreographic contest of barbaric intensity in which the hero, Tariel, defeated his opponent, Avtandil.

Ballet Theatre (later American Ballet Theatre) opened at Covent Garden on, appropriately, 4 July: an exciting company both for its dancers and for its ballets. Cyril wrote delightedly of Jerome Robbins's 'hair-trigger sense of timing' in *Fancy Free*, and found Tudor's *Pillar of Fire*

> a work of unusual interest and importance… another attempt of Tudor's to use Dance for a higher purpose than that of providing mere visual entertainment… [He] succeeds very well in showing us the warring emotions, the jarred nerves and varied tensions of mind resulting from this tangle of frustrated lives.

The Dancing Times in January 1946 reproduced a photograph of a statue of Pavlova by G.F. Paulin that it was proposed to put up at Ivy House, where she had lived in London. The Sitter Out remarked that, since completing the model, Paulin had discussed it with Ruth French (a *première danseuse* in Pavlova's company) and had made some alterations to the face and head. A letter from Cyril was published in April, welcoming the idea of a memorial but deploring the design:

> It lacks that elegance, expressiveness and style which were so characteristic of her dancing. And why should she be poised standing on the head of a swan, the position of whose neck is scarcely a tribute to the dancer's grace and lightness? Finally, nothing could be more incongruous than a dancer in a short ballet skirt without tights or ballet shoes.

Four books were published in 1946. *Ballet Design Past and Present* combined and extended the two previous books on design, *Design for the Ballet* (1937) and *Five Centuries of Ballet Design* (1939), covering the evolution of design from the Italian Renaissance to 'the present day'. Cyril wrote a long and scholarly introduction to the volume, plus valuable captions to the illustrated designs that ran from Jacques Patin's for the *Ballet Comique de la Reine* (1581) to John Piper's for Ashton's *The Quest* in 1943. The other three books were *The Sleeping Beauty* (about the Sadler's Wells Ballet 1946 Covent Garden production), for which Cyril wrote the text; *The Sadler's Wells Ballet*; and *Leslie Hurry: Settings and Costumes for Sadler's Wells Ballet. The Sadler's Wells Ballet*, dedicated to 'Those of my Friends, Past or Present Members of the Sadler's Wells Ballet', was described by him as an account of the principal productions in the permanent repertoire. It dealt with the pre-Fokine ballets, the Fokine ballets, and ballets by de Valois, Ashton, Helpmann and Andrée Howard (who had choreographed only *The Spider's Banquet* for them at that time). He pointed out in his Preface that, as so much had been written about the leading dancers and soloists, he had concentrated on descriptions of the ballets and short historical or critical comments. One ballet that he would have liked to include, Ashton's *A Wedding Bouquet*, was omitted because, surprisingly enough, he had never seen it. *The Dancing Times* review called it 'a very valuable book of reference, and though one may not always agree with the author's critical remarks, these are certainly worthy of most careful consideration'.

In the Leslie Hurry book, he discussed Hurry's designs for Helpmann's ballet *Hamlet* (1942) and for *Swan Lake* (1943). The designs for Hamlet commanded his admiration. The scenery, an extraordinary conception, which positively vibrates with a dynamic rhythm, is certainly the most original setting for ballet seen in recent years. Mysterious, ominous, and filled with a sense of open and lurking menace, few spectators can look upon it for the first time without an involuntary catch of the breath.

The costumes were also praised, the dual nature of characters (as envisaged by Helpmann) being brilliantly achieved with asymmetrical sleeves and splendid colours. *Swan Lake* was 'a brilliantly lit fantasia on the swan theme' but did not achieve the complete success of the *Hamlet*. 'None the less, it is clear that Hurry is an artist of remarkable abilities and extraordinary imaginative powers which at times recall the prophetic visions of William Blake.'

Cyril continued to review regularly for Buckle's *Ballet*. In 1947 he covered the Sadler's Wells Ballet's latest production of *Le Lac des cygnes* (only later did Britain universally translate the title into *Swan Lake*) and, typically, he singled out supporting dancers for praise. He decided that 'it would be difficult to find a better Benno' than Leslie Edwards, 'whose stage manners are impeccable, always friendly, courteous and gracious but never presuming on the Prince's friendship', while Paul Reymond's Wolfgang was also liked: '[He] suggests over-indulgence in wine without ever being vulgar.' It is not every critic, alas, who treats lesser roles with as much respect as leads. In dealing with Odette-Odile as danced by Moira Shearer and Beryl Grey, he was acute. He praised Shearer's musical sensitivity, her grace and style, but felt that her dancing at this point was 'what the French call *style boudoir*... her arm movements are too restricted and the whole presentation too dainty'. Grey had 'an excellent sense of line... speed, vigour and the buoyancy of youth', although her Odette needed more lyricism and poetry.

In the March/April number, Cyril had the chance to write about Massine's notable engagement with the Sadler's Wells Ballet, when de Valois invited him to stage and dance the leads in *Le Tricorne* and *La Boutique fantasque*. As Cyril wrote:

> Every lover of ballet must applaud the leadership and foresight which prompted these two steps, since they enabled the company to add two popular Massine works to their repertory; gave English dancers an opportunity of working under one of the great choreographers of the century; and afforded contemporary English audiences a chance of seeing Massine in action.

The notice was ideally framed, beginning, as Cyril had more right than most to do, by recapping the background to the first productions of the two ballets and the impression they made at the time, then going on to assess the revivals. The scenery for *Tricorne* was dingy and faded, but the costumes 'made a brave show and the dancing has both pace and zest, although it lacks the depth and lilt and varying "colour" which Russian dancers contrive to infuse into their movements and steps'. He mentioned differences. Massine, 'wisely aware that a quarter of a century is bound to affect a dancer's strength', had pruned his role. 'The Farucca, originally danced in a wide ellipse, has been considerably curtailed.' He was, however, still a fine artist and even in its condensed form the Farucca 'does not fail to thrill the house'.

Other choreographic details were mentioned. Violetta Prokhorova [Elvin] had vitality but lacked variety of mood; John Hart's Corregidor was compared, to his disadvantage, with Woizikovsky's: Hart was an 'oafish sensualist' where Woizikovsky was 'a cunning, vicious old nobleman... a figure at once fascinating and repulsive'. Alexander Grant as the Dandy fared best, having a sparkling gaiety, but he, too, failed to achieve 'the combination of mockery and insolence with which Idzikovski invested the role'.

In *Boutique*, again the setting was dingy, and (as seems inevitable with all revivals) costume colours were often wrong. Cyril was not unkind to the Sadler's Wells dancers but pointed out that the original artists of the first rank 'had been in the main replaced by young dancers of talent and promise'. However, he praised (and I would agree with him) the excellent conception of Alexis Rassine as the Snob. Massine's Can-Can Dancer had naturally lost something of 'the sinuous movement and cat-like tread' that it used to possess, while Moira Shearer's pretty and attractive Can-Can Dancer lacked the vitality and high spirits of Lopokova's.

For the June number, Cyril concentrated on Sally Gilmour. Once again, the article was a model of critical format. He had chosen to write of her because she had never had the publicity devoted to Fonteyn or Shearer, and yet she had

> three solid achievements to her credit and she is endowed with that most rare and coveted gift among dancers, the quality of expression, without which dancing can achieve no more than the perfection of a machine or the supreme but cold beauty of a superb style.

He detailed her background and training. Unusually, it was her father, a bacteriologist, rather than her mother, who had envisaged her as a ballerina and planned her education to that end. She became a student of Karsavina and later Rambert. Cyril went on to analyse her ability as a dance-actress, instancing creations such as Andrée Howard's *Lady into Fox* and Walter Gore's *Confessional*, and her achievement as Giselle. She was versatile and 'equally at home with either the comic or the tragic muse'. Of her Giselle he wrote that in his view it was 'unequalled by any English dancer of her generation for its lyric qualities, its poetry, its pathos. Other interpreters of the role may excel her in technical ability, but not one of them equals her in expression.' In summing up, he described her personality as 'enigmatic and elusive, as though she mused over things known to herself alone… Her expression is as changeable as the face of nature; now smiling, now aglow with child-like rapture, now radiant with some inner ecstasy of the spirit'.

The articles that Cyril contributed to *Ballet* form a valuable series. In July 1947 he dealt with *La Sylphide*, which the Ballets des Champs-Élysées had just shown London in the Boris Kochno/Victor Gsovsky reconstruction of Filippo Taglioni's version. Once again the historical context was detailed and then the background to the new staging explained and its performance analysed. In total he welcomed the production, which was 'the fruit of long and ardent research combined with a refined taste and an abiding love for that epoch which gave birth to the *ballet blanc*'. At the end he threw in the tantalising thought that other choreographers might use the material: 'the plot of *La Sylphide* will support a dozen different choreographic versions'. Cyril was never an enemy of novel ideas; he only opposed, as strongly as he could, all alterations to existing works that distorted their original character.

He had plenty of examples of this to deal with when Colonel de Basil's Original Ballet Russe staged their first post-war London season at Covent Garden that July, and he dealt with them in the September number of *Ballet*. The new company admittedly lacked a great classical ballerina, and the *corps de ballet* did not have the essential homogeneity possible only with a seasoned team of dancers. Examining the revivals in detail, however, he could find nothing but unacceptable choreographic changes and altered emphases in interpretation. No ballet measured up well, in his view, to its original state, and one, *Schéhérazade*, 'is so different from what it once was that, if it cannot be presented with taste and artistry, it is better to relegate it to oblivion'.

In other articles that year he fell back on research topics, rather than criticising current events. In August he wrote about Auguste Vestris. In October he produced a fascinating study of the Horse Ballets of the seventeenth century, and in November his subject was Simon Slingsby, 'the first English dancer to achieve eminence both sides of the Channel'.

Cyril returned to topical subjects in January 1948 with an article about the Sadler's Wells Ballet's revival of de Valois's *Checkmate* and Massine's production of *Mam'zelle Angot*. For *Checkmate* some of the costumes were new and less effective, but he admired de Valois's choreography, which had 'a sense of mathematical construction in which the music has been carefully studied and scientifically translated into choreographic terms'. The main weakness was

> the new treatment of the role of the Red King, who once added much to the interest and intensity of the fatal duel between the Black Queen and the Red Knight by vividly reflecting in his movements the swaying fortunes of the contest. As now presented the Red King is so stylised as to contribute little or nothing of dramatic value to the ballet.

The explanation was that in this revival the Red King was not danced by its creator, Robert Helpmann. In later years he returned to the role and restored to it the intensity Cyril mentions. Pamela May, he found, danced and mimed the Black Queen with great effect, although she was 'a vengeful Medusa-like figure' rather than June Brae's original sultry, voluptuous queen.

Mam'zelle Angot was a revised version of a ballet composed by Massine for Ballet Theatre. Cyril found it a relief, after psychologically intense ballets, 'to be able to sit back and enjoy the dancing and miming'. Fonteyn in the title role, Shearer as the Aristocrat, Michael Somes as the Caricaturist and Alexander Grant as the Barber all danced admirably, even if 'a quick-tempered soubrette' was not really Fonteyn's forte. His estimate of the acts entirely chimes with my recollection: 'as regards the choreography, Act I is excellent, Act II is good, but Act III is still untidy and uncertain in design'. It remained that way.

More research pieces ensued, about the father and son Vestris (March 1948), on postcards of the Imperial Russian Ballet (April), and a very lively piece about a colourful dancer of the 1820s, Maria Mercandotti (May). In October, the month that saw the magazine's title change to *Ballet and Opera*, he reviewed the season of the Grand Ballet de Monte Carlo, directed by the Marquis de Cuevas. He saw Balanchine's *Concerto Barocco*, which he found admirably phrased to the music. But he felt that 'the dancers have the air of being the units of an elaborate piece of smooth-running clockwork rather than human beings. Thus the ballet has an astringent, impersonal, robot-like quality.'

A revival of *Les Biches*, compared with the original, was 'quite innocuous', and he did not much care for Nijinska's *Brahms Variations*, but enjoyed Antonia Cobos's *Mute Wife*, which was presented with 'wit and a real appreciation of the development of the action. Although its choreographic range is limited and the action conveyed more in terms of mime than in terms of expressive dancing, none the less it is both competent and amusing.'

He was also impressed by Balanchine's *Night Shadow*, which had 'all the romantic atmosphere and the sudden change from joy to tragedy of a tale by Pushkin'. The celebrated sleepwalking dance was performed 'with feeling and restraint by [Ethery] Pagava…

admirably supported by [George] Skibine'. Typically, Cyril threw in a few thoughts at the end. He found that even the principals (Rosella Hightower, Maria Tallchief and André Eglevsky) seemed to be limited in their appreciation of style-atmosphere.

> They execute the most difficult steps with a surprising ease. They dazzle with their brilliance. But there is little genuine atmosphere, little real feeling behind the movements. One is entertained but rarely moved, and one goes home filled with a sense of disappointment and dissatisfaction. I speak, of course, for myself; it may be that others feel quite differently.

In addition, he noted how choreography 'was tending to become nothing more than the exploitation of some technical facilities peculiar to certain dancers', and that some steps were used to excess and indiscriminately. 'Acrobatics can serve dancing, but we must beware lest they become its master.'

In November he reverted to the Ballets des Champs-Élysées, this year without Roland Petit. He was glad to find that *Le Jeune Homme et la mort* remained 'the masterpiece it has always been', with Jean Babilée and Nathalie Philippart giving inspired performances. Babilée was described as superb, an adjective sparingly used by Cyril: 'His movements have a rare beauty, partly from his masterly execution and partly from his delicate sense of line and his admirable timing, which I personally find most inspiring.' *Le Rendez-vous* also held its own, although Youly Algaroff replaced Petit as the Young Man. Babilée and Philippart again danced the Hunchback and the Beautiful Girl, and Jean Blanchard's Destiny had improved so much that the role, which 'formerly seemed introduced merely to provide a touch of the macabre, is now vital to the action in its immense power'.

The interesting new works included Aurel Milloss's *Portrait de Don Quichotte* and David Lichine's *La Création*. The Milloss ballet, a short dance-drama about a man who wanted to relive Quixote's adventures, was all make-believe, a string of episodes taking place in a curtained booth. Cyril liked its 'resource and ingenuity in suggesting the adventures in terms of dance and mime with an unusual economy of means'. The ballet rested totally on Babilée, whose 'noble bearing and air of one possessed are so convincing in their utter sincerity that the most incredible happenings seem quite natural'.

Advance publicity for *La Création* had claimed that it was 'a ballet without music, without scenery, and without costumes, which last might have caused the Lord Chamberlain to lift a questioning eyebrow'. Cyril, however, felt it was not so much a ballet without music, as a ballet before music. He went on to dissect Lichine's talent, with which he had been familiar for many years. Lichine, he stressed,

> carries music within him. Like Jeanne d'Arc he hears voices, but of another kind – strong rhythms and light rhythms which people his mind with vague forms which grow clearer, form patterns, dissolve and fade, and emerge again to form some new design… To give them life the choreographer needs human bodies.

This method of choreographic composition was the Creation of the title. Cyril obviously found it fascinating: 'We seem not to be watching a ballet but, concealed by the surrounding darkness, to be viewing in secret the performance of some mysterious mystic rite.'

Mona Inglesby's International Ballet was Cyril's task for December. He dealt with *Swan Lake*, *Coppélia* and *The Sleeping Princess*, being underwhelmed by them all. *Dances from Prince Igor* was an unsatisfactory version arranged by Ivanov 'presumably for some production of Borodin's opera'. Cyril was dry about it:

It is asking a great deal to expect four warriors and their chief to suggest a Polovtsian horde… there is a tendency to indulge in too much lashing of the ground with bows; a little is in character, an excess suggests the more peaceable pursuit of carpet-beating.

In 1948 Ashton had been active, staging *Don Juan* (November) and *Cinderella* (December) for the Sadler's Wells Ballet. *Don Juan* had

almost all the qualities some modern audiences seem to require of a ballet. It is clever, smart, slick, up to the minute in choreographic fashions, but although it undoubtedly has moments of fitful brilliance, as a whole I find it unsatisfying.

Cinderella, described in immense detail, was compared with the Soviet and the earlier Petipa versions. Its importance was that it was the first full-length academic ballet to be composed by an English choreographer. It was, however, uneven. There was a shortage of dances for men, apart from the Jester. Cinderella had some charming solos and *pas de deux*, but 'the prime interest of the ballet is centred upon the Ugly Sisters'. The Fairies of the Seasons were full of interest and invention; and in spite of any weaknesses *Cinderella* was an undoubted success. Cyril, in fact, turned good prophet: 'This ballet will surely pass into the permanent repertory and give rise to a long line of Cinderellas.'

Cyril had sent de Valois a telegram of good wishes. He was constantly wiring dancers or choreographers, something much appreciated by the recipients. De Valois replied:

It certainly was an exciting occasion. I have been saying for 18 months that the moment had arrived when the English Ballet must consider the possibility of a full length production. In many ways it is the answer to this large Opera House. The technical approach of composers, choreographers and scenario writers will be important... the one-act ballet leads to a technique... that in its brevity invariably becomes monotonously highly stylised, purely abstract, or (in the cases where a story is involved) the action is reduced to too much mime. You may gather from this letter that I want to turn over a fresh page in our history.

In February 1949 Petit's Ballets de Paris arrived, with its famous *Carmen*, and Cyril had no hesitation in declaring that this ballet 'as a conception for the theatre... is superb. Vigorous, racy, dramatic, it glows and throbs with passion... with the tact, skill and artistry of Jeanmaire and Petit, it is a masterpiece of emotional experience.' The repertoire also included Petit's cat ballet, *Les Demoiselles de la nuit*, 'charming in both conception and realisation'. *L'Oeuf à la cocque* 'would make the fortune of a revue', but was out of place in a ballet programme; William Dollar's *Le Combat* needed editing and shortening.

In August, Cyril covered Le Grand Ballet de Monte Carlo. Most of the repertoire was as before. A revival of *The Good-Humoured Ladies*, even as staged by Massine himself, was a profound disappointment. New designs by André Derain were a mistake, and there were choreographic changes for the worse; Cyril could only echo Villon's lament, *Ou sont les neiges d'antan?* *Le Beau Danube* was much better, more or less as it was conceived, with Desormière's orchestration and with a reasonable approximation of the original costumes. Massine still gave a remarkable performance, for his age, as the Hussar; Riabouchinska remained the most charming of exponents as the Young Girl; but Rosella Hightower, although an executant of rare ability, failed with the Street Dancer.

Ballet and Opera in September 1949 dwelt very much on the twentieth anniversary of Diaghilev's death, and Cyril once more wrote about his dancers; but in November he reverted to the Ballets des Champs-Élysées. The novelty was *La Rencontre*, a ballet by Lichine on the theme of Oedipus and the Sphinx, to music by Sauguet. It was very well arranged and often exciting, a 'happy blending of the antique and modern', dramatic movement and mime rather than dancing. The Sphinx was Leslie Caron –'half feline, half feminine… admirably timed and phrased' – and Babilée, for whom Cyril (rightly) continued to feel the utmost admiration, was Oedipus.

The only book Cyril published in 1949 was an anthology of his reviews, *Dancers Under My Lens*, which began with extracts from *The Dancing World*. Although in 1950 he was appointed dance critic for the *Sunday Times*, he continued to write occasionally for *Ballet and Opera*, for which he reviewed de Valois's last major ballet, *Don Quixote*, staged by Sadler's Wells Ballet in February 1950. He felt it an almost impossible task to make a serious ballet out of Cervantes's book, but he was 'impressed by the cleverness and ingenuity with which [she] has striven to overcome the innate difficulties of her task'. He remarked on picturesque and well-contrived groupings and several moving incidents, but missed the romantic element and deplored the preponderance of mime and dramatised movement over pure dancing. He praised Helpmann's

> restrained, dignified and often moving interpretation… This dignity is imperative, for it is precisely this quality added to his obvious sincerity… that make Don Quixote's fantastic behaviour inspire sympathy and pity rather than ridicule. There are several episodes which could so easily become an excuse for farce, but Helpmann always resists this temptation and keeps strictly to character.

There was also wholehearted praise for Alexander Grant's

Sancho Panza, 'an excellent performance which never flags despite its arduous nature'.

The 1950s began well for Cyril. When in 1950 France awarded him the Croix de Chevalier de la Légion d'Honneur for his research on ballet in Paris, among the congratulations he received was a letter from Marie Rambert: 'It gives me real pleasure to learn of your honour. You are, if anybody, a *chevalier sans peur et sans reproche*, and though in title you will belong to a Legion there are in fact far too few who are your peers.' From 1951 to 1961 he was chairman of the Ballet Section of the Critics' Circle (and president of the Circle itself in 1957) and he continued to contribute to *Ballet* (as it had become again) until it ceased publication in 1952. During 1950 he wrote for Buckle about the Nijinsky Galas – programmes of arena ballet staged in London's Empress Hall, when dancers like Markova and Dolin, Massine, Toumanova and Babilée were supported by Ballet Rambert. Other articles were on the Characters in *Swan Lake* and on Roland Petit's *Ballabile* for Sadler's Wells Ballet. As dance critic for the *Sunday Times* he had to learn a new style – writing reviews for a newspaper is a completely different discipline from writing articles and books, and Cyril became very proficient at meeting the requirements for length of the period (British papers were much smaller than they now are). With this Sunday slot in which to cover the dance events of each week, for nine years he reviewed ballet, contemporary dance, ethnic dance, dance films, dance in pantomimes, mime and puppetry.

His attitude to his work was set out in an essay, dedicated to Fonteyn, that he contributed to an anthology, *Dancers and Critics*, edited that year by Cyril Swinson. Criticism, he declared, was 'the examination of a choreographic work in the light of an informed taste which is part intellectual and part emotional', and he went on to dissect in detail the qualities needed by a critic.

Responses and styles of writing had to be varied for different kinds of productions. A critic had to understand traditional ballets but be 'equally receptive to new ideas in choreography', and should have a knowledge of the history of ballet, art, literature and music. He then went on to discuss the critical evaluation of performers and the ethics of ballet criticism.

It was about this time that Jill Anne Bowden went to work for Cyril at the shop. Her job, described as secretarial assistant, was wide-ranging and in the end covered proofreading, indexing and considerable editorial duties. She remembers how his *Sunday Times* articles were always originally three times as long as the published pieces – he compressed and reworded and omitted, always wondering, Does it give an impression? Would it give anybody the idea? 'He sought to evoke images in the mind which would create for the reader something of the experience of ballet.' About his way of working, Jill Anne writes that he always began slowly, warmed up as his concentration deepened, and then could go on for ten or twelve hours without evidence of fatigue. She also stresses his 'total independence of judgement, his fidelity to his own response… other influences never imposed upon him':

> He was invariably courteous: but he never courted anyone, never sought to ingratiate himself with another, however eminent. A political or advantageous friendship would have been unthinkable to him.

The wide coverage for the *Sunday Times* was demonstrated in January 1951, when he wrote about one fairy play, *Where the Rainbow Ends*, and three typical Christmas pantomimes, *Mother Goose*, *Goody Two Shoes* and *Babes in the Wood*. He made the point that where ballet in musical shows had 'immensely improved, thanks to the inspiring models provided by Agnes de Mille and Michael Kidd', ballet in pantomime had almost ceased to exist. In November he covered Mrinalini Sarabhai in three classic Indian styles and Pearl Primus in an African and Afro-American programme, *Dark Rhythms*. Asian and African dancers always interested him. He greatly enjoyed the Spanish duo Rosario and Antonio, who were dancing better than ever, and described Antonio eloquently:

> His infectious charm captivates his audience... he carries within him a whole vocabulary of subtle and intricate rhythms... his Zapateado to the music of Sarasate remains his outstanding achievement as virtuoso... What strength and control are needed to feed such fluctuating fires of movement!

Other reviews dealt with such dancers as Pilar Lopez and Carmen Amaya.

Another outlet for writers on dance during this period was *The Ballet Annual*, a yearbook published in London and initially edited by Arnold Haskell; in due course editorial teams included Cyril Swinson with G.B.L. Wilson, and Mary Clarke with Ivor Guest. As an occasional contributor, Cyril covered the London Archives of the Dance in the opening issue and later wrote about Markova and Dolin, Zizi Jeanmaire, Adolph Bolm, a televised *Sleeping Beauty*, Fonteyn and (inevitably) Cecchetti. The most poignant was his description of Nijinsky's funeral on 14 April 1950. He had been one of the pallbearers, along with Ashton, Buckle, Dolin, Lifar and Michael Somes. The requiem mass took place in London at St James's Church, Spanish Place. The church was crowded with mourners, the service was long, and

> above the altar the stained glass windows, like a jewelled mosaic of ruby and sapphire, alternately glowed and flamed as the sun outside shone through them or was dimmed by a

passing cloud. Lifar rose, and walked from his pew carrying a wreath of primroses which he laid on the floor just before the head of the coffin.

The coffin was immensely heavy and the strength of the six men was severely taxed. The roof of the hearse was a mass of wreaths and posies; the steps of the church and the nearby pavements were packed with people. The principal mourners went on to St Mary's Cemetery on Finchley Road for the burial. The priest conducted a service and Romola Nijinsky scattered some roses into the grave. Lifar and Cyril sprinkled a little earth on the coffin, and as they left, Cyril looked back and saw Ram Gopal, the great Indian dancer, standing alone by the grave. Cyril had first seen Nijinsky in 1912:

> I little thought then, as I watched that wonderful youth dance, the great artist who had certainly acquired a stature akin to a god among ordinary earthbound mortals, that some thirty-eight years later I should be one of those destined to bear him to his final resting-place.

He then summed up in a companion article, *Garland for Nijinsky*, the special qualities that had made him great:

> With grease paint and nose-paste and false hair, the skilled dancer can do much to achieve a change of appearance. But Nijinsky's assumption of a role went far deeper. It was not only the face, the façade, that changed, but the mind and personality behind it which altered. The change was not skin-deep, but soul-deep… He could play upon movement in the same way that a great actor clothes words, now with fire, now with the most melting tenderness.

During 1951 Cyril wrote reviews for *Ballet* on Herbert Ross's *Caprichos*, four casts of *Giselle*, Cullberg's Swedish Ballet and John Cranko's *Pineapple Poll*. For the *Sunday Times*, he took the occasion of another De Cuevas Ballet visit to set out some points on which he felt strongly. He criticised designs: 'Is a designer chosen simply for being in vogue at the moment? Or because he or she can make a valuable contribution to the presentation of a ballet?', and reiterated his strongly held views about technique and expressiveness:

> Are dancers to use their technical equipment as a means of expression or are they intended to be no more than wonderful pieces of human machinery – live puppets?... The latter is fast becoming the ideal. The dancer who can turn the greatest number of pirouettes with precision, who can spin in the air the most times, or who can jump the highest, would appear to be valued far more than the dancer who has the artistry to convey in terms of movement a mood, a situation, or a particular period.

He went on to another point, that of the tendency to 'edit' the classic ballets:

> What would be said of a musical director who cut movements from a Beethoven symphony because he felt that they did not accord with present-day conceptions of music? Yet one constantly sees phrases of mime excised, dances altered, beautiful flowing movements replaced by ugly staccato ones, and the works thus 'improved' are still presented as *Les Sylphides* or *Le Lac des Cygnes*.

Cyril continued to correspond with the Leslies, who had not yet returned to Europe. His letter of 26 January 1951 reported that before Christmas 1950 Alice had fallen rather badly in the street, breaking both her wrists and a bone in her hand, but was at last going on well. A year later, according to his 28 January 1952 letter, she was again in trouble with an acute attack of sciatica and had to stay in bed most of the day:

> What with trying to be nurse and cook, and running between times to the shop, it has all been most difficult. However, after working at it on and off for five years, I have completed my study of *Swan Lake* which may be printed in three or four months… I have also written a little impression of Antonio which should be ready some time this year [both were indeed published by him in 1952].

The heavy demands upon his time notwithstanding, Cyril regularly continued to cover all kinds of dance events for the *Sunday Times*. Katherine Dunham's group appeared in January 1952 and won an accolade as 'a most talented company… Miss Dunham, as choreographer, unites originality, a rare feeling for atmosphere, and a fine sense of the theatre.' A year later the English Folk Dance and Song Society were evaluated – Cyril particularly liked the Ravensbourne Morris group, 'with its excellent fool and hobby-horse with a doggish sense of humour', and the curious old Abbots Bromley Horn Dance, in which the dancers 'stole softly over the ground in semi-obscurity like some ghostly homage to Herne the Hunter'.

Sadler's Wells Ballet put on yet another new production of *Swan Lake* in December 1952. Cyril talked about it beforehand with de Valois and sent her a copy of his new book, *The Ballet Called Swan Lake*. She replied, thanking him for 'publishing the book just at the right moment!' and writing in great detail about her plans for the production. These included a much fuller production of Act I: she was putting twelve men into the peasants' dance and changing the musical cut in the middle, reinstating all the mime, and re-setting the little peasant girl's solo with the *pas de six* – purposely rather classical. In Act II she had put back the 32 swans and 'lengthened musically the scene where the Prince attempts to shoot von Rothbart (it was a bad, abrupt cut in the music)'. In Act III there would be a cloud of vapours to cover the exit of von Rothbart, while the Prince would 'disappear through the same on a wild rush from the palace'. In Act IV she had put back 'some very nice music in the opening number, and the necessary bit of the storm music, which should be there as the proper build up for the Prince's entrance'. She concluded, 'The problem of the final scene is not yet definite in my mind… well, I will know by the end of the week!'

The Ballet Called Swan Lake was dedicated 'To Natalie René (Roslavleva), in Gratitude and Friendship', and the preface explained why:

> It would have been almost impossible for me to describe the early productions of *Swan Lake* without the help of a Russian friend, Miss Natalie René (Moscow), an assiduous student of Ballet, who not only most generously aided me in the acquisition of Russian documentation but also frequently suggested fruitful sources of study. This book owes a great deal to her unremitting interest and her constant encouragement over several years.

There are a good many letters from Roslavleva (her professional name) in the Beaumont Collection at the Theatre Museum, London, typed on both sides of airmail-weight paper that has not aged well. Information of every kind pours out in her extremely fluent writing style; one might almost term it an *embarras de richesses*. Fancifully, following some little private joke, she addresses Cyril for the most part as Dear Doctor Coppélius and refers to herself as Lilac Fairy. Once, because he had evidently requested more detail about something, he is addressed as Dear Mr Micawber. Their association probably started around 1947, when she must have applied to him for information – on 2 February 1948, she remarks how much he had helped her with her thesis about Didelot, so their exchange of research information must have been mutual.

In the August 1952 *Ballet*, Cyril's article was about the New York City Ballet season, when Robbins's *The Cage* was given. He described it as basically a long *pas de deux*, as the *corps de ballet* work was slight, and even suggested an old-fashioned revue. The *pas de deux* itself, however, was another matter:

> Although extremely acrobatic, it is novel and cleverly composed. It has flow, but bristles with technical difficulties… Although some of the movements are ugly and repugnant, and at times even in questionable taste, the ballet is strongly dramatic… Nora Kaye gives an impressive interpretation of the aggressive and ruthless Novice.

The Bolshoi Ballet as a company reached London only in 1956, but some Soviet dancers appeared during 1953 and 1954 in concerts arranged in connection with a visit by a Soviet delegation. They included Alla Shelest, Konstantin Shatilov, Raissa Struchkova and Alexander Lapauri, but Cyril was not very impressed by them. In his reviews he commented on faults of style and presentation as well as appalling costumes and acrobatic choreography:

> It was certainly breathtaking to see Struchkova launch herself like a human rocket aimed horizontally at her partner, to be dextrously caught by him, tossed in the air, and swung vertically upwards… their acrobatic dancing was dazzling in its speed, precision and delicate balance. It would, however, be of greater interest to see such dancers in true ballet.

Cyrll Beaumont with the Danish ballerina Kirsten Simone.

Late summer of 1953 saw the first visit to Britain of the Royal Danish Ballet, which Cyril greatly admired and had seen on its home ground in Copenhagen. Travel abroad (apart from Paris) figured little in his life, mainly because of Alice's increasing and chronic physical troubles and his reluctance to leave her without his support. The Danish Ballet returned to the Edinburgh Festival in 1955 and Cyril saw them there. They repeated *La Sylphide*, and Cyril wrote with great admiration of Margrethe Schanne's 'poetical interpretation... I cannot conceive the role being better done. Schanne is matched in artistry by Gerda Karstens' sinister portrait of Madge.' They also showed Ashton's recently staged *Romeo and Juliet*, which Cyril found to be a true choreographic poem. 'What impresses one most about the ballet is the clarity of statement and the adroit manner in which lyrical mime is fused with dance. One need not know Shakespeare to understand the actions.' Henning Kronstam was noble and romantic-looking, dancing and miming with passion, while Mona Vangsaa gave an inspired performance with a subtle sense of situation. In *Napoli*, with its last-act 'non-stop kaleidoscopic succession of beautifully contrasted dances', Vangsaa was partnered by Børge Ralov.

It was during the Danes' 1953 London season that a young Danish dancer, Kirsten Simone, had made her debut in *A Folk Tale*. She was receiving special training from someone Cyril knew well, Vera Volkova, and he offered to pay the fees for these classes. He must have written in 1955 to suggest that it was time he did this again, for Volkova replied that it was not necessary, as the coaching was now part of her regular work. Cyril obviously kept this in mind, because in 1960 he was in touch with the Royal Theatre in Copenhagen about establishing an annual scholarship for a promising young member of the Royal Danish Ballet. This was set up, and each year he was told to which student it had been awarded. The first one, in 1962, was given to Eske Holm, and among later names appear Peter Schaufuss, Johnny Eliasen, Adam Lüders and Mette-Ida Kirk. Schaufuss's letter of thanks (he was less familiar with English when he was eighteen) reads:

> I became very happy to receive it. It is so encouraging to a young artist to know that people appreciate his work. I am happy because it is an acknowledgement and I may do my best to prove that I was it worth. The reason why this letter has not come until now is that I wanted to send you a picture which I have just got today.

Cyril had, in fact, promoted a pilot scheme of this kind in 1950. That year he founded a René Blum Prize, to be given annually by a panel of French critics to the most promising young French dancer of the year. It continued until 1968, and the list of winners includes Claire Sombert in 1952, Georges Piletta in 1961, and Noella Pontois in 1964. In 1974 Cyril proposed putting the Danish scholarship on a permanent basis by an investment of capital in Danish securities. Over the years he had also always included a small sum to pay for a laurel wreath to be placed on the theatre's bust of Bournonville at the annual May Festival.

The London Museum marked the fifteenth anniversary of Pavlova's death in 1956 with a commemorative exhibition. Cyril wrote of it in the *Sunday Times*, singling out exhibits such as Sir John Lavery's vivid painting of *Autumn Bacchanale* and Bakst's fine drawing of her, 'the best of all likenesses'. In other rooms were her costume for Act I of *Giselle* and the shroud-like dress she wore in Act II; her pink bonnet, muff and cloak from *Christmas*; and her costume for *The Dying Swan*. The exhibition was 'a model of its kind, presented with such taste and reverence that it becomes doubly moving'.

In July 1957 Cyril went to Bristol to see Western Theatre Ballet, a newly formed company that planned to present original works with a narrative-dramatic element. He was immediately pleased with Peter Darrell's *The Prisoners*, set to Bartok's *Music for Celeste, Percussion and Strings*, which had a very strong story about two escaped convicts: 'The action is conveyed more in dramatic movement than actual steps, but the work is good theatre and readily understood.' London's Festival Ballet (later

London Festival Ballet and now English National Ballet) was then at the Royal Festival Hall, where he saw a new Lichine ballet, *Concerti*, which disappointed him as being 'mainly a series of classroom exercises… the general effect is of mechanism rather than art'. It was a curtain raiser to *Giselle*, in which guest artist Liane Daydé from Paris was partnered by John Gilpin. Daydé had

> an engaging vivacity and a brilliant technique, particularly in batterie, pirouettes and travelled turns. She mimes well, investing the love scenes with tenderness. She is equally good in the Mad Scene, offering a very personal and mainly muted conception.

Letters to and from the Leslies continued sporadically. In January 1957 Cyril was apologising for having nothing new of his own to send them:

> Whether it is that I am getting old or lazy, I do not know, but while I have several plans for books and have toyed with various ideas, I have accomplished very little in the way of new books. We must see what this year brings forth.

Instead, he sent them *The Moscow Bolshoi Theatre Ballet*, a book produced for the 1956 Covent Garden season. About the company Cyril commented:

> They have some very good dancers but the choreography is very old-fashioned, in the main pre-Diaghilev, except for some acrobatic lifts and a step like splits in the air, of which they are very fond and introduce on the slightest provocation. Ulanova is very good indeed, with a wonderfully fluid body.

The previous October, in a *Sunday Times* review, he had raised some relevant points about the Bolshoi's production of *Giselle* by Leonid Lavrovsky (as opposed to Ulanova's performance). He liked the fact that in Act I, 'when the Duke seeks refreshment, his squire directs retainers to help Giselle and her mother to bring out table and chairs, a vast improvement on the normal procedure when a dozen girls emerge from a tiny cottage'. Why, however, did Hilarion carry a gun in the Middle Ages? Why did Bathilde wear a dress of white satin and gold brocade to go hunting? Why did one mime artist squire both Albrecht and the Duke? And why, at the end of Act I, was Giselle allowed to take a curtain call? His pertinent queries continued in Act II. Why were the Wilis pink-cheeked, or was this a tribute to the embalmer's art? Why, in the invocation scene, were the Wilis grouped upstage when Giselle's grave was placed downstage? Why, in the finale, did Albrecht embrace Giselle, refuting the illusion that she is a vision? How often a dance critic longs to list just such a number of questions about ballet productions!

Cyril's next letter to the Leslies told them more about the London Archives of the Dance. He had continued to be chairman, but Deryck Lynham had died very suddenly in Lausanne in 1951 and Lionel Bradley in 1953, so it fell to Cyril to make all decisions. He now brought Serge Leslie up to date, telling him how everything had been in abeyance because of a lack of funds 'to hire a room or two to start it'. Now, after 12 years of disappointment, he had been promised a small flat to house the collection, and they hoped to open it to the public for a few hours each week or fortnight. This never happened. In August 1958 he thanked Serge for a donation he had sent for the Archives, and mentioned that he was working on a book about puppets that should be ready in October.

Ever since April 1957 the Leslies had been in touch with Cyril concerning a book about Doris Niles that Serge had written. On receipt of the typescript, Cyril wrote that he 'would very much like Serge to see his book in print'. He would be happy to prepare the book for press, and I could get it printed and bound, but to put the book on the market would be difficult for me. I could only do this in the rather haphazard way I have to publish my own books. On the other hand, I have an American agent who would be able to sell a number of copies. [This was Al Pischl of the Dance Mart in New York.] I think it would be difficult to sell here because it is a long time since you [Doris Niles] danced in London and you would be little known to the present generation of balletgoers. Of course in America the position would be different.

He went on to say, 'The actual cost of printing would be high. Printing now is about four times what it was before the war and binding is about four or five times higher… Paper, too, is horribly dear.' However, the arrangements went ahead. Cyril was unhappy with a proposed title, *American Gypsy* (it might suggest a travel book) and put forward the suggestion of *Life is a Dance* 'but perhaps this is rather Martha Grahamish' or *My Life is Dancing*, with a subtitle 'an account of the career and friends of Doris Niles'. In the end it appeared in 1958 with the title *The Seven Leagues of a Dancer*, with the subtitle 'being an account of the career of Doris Niles'. It was the second book about Niles, as in 1937 Cyril had published *Doris Niles: Interpreter of the Spanish Dance*, by Cornelius Conyn.

Cyril had been vice-chairman of the ISTD for some thirteen years when, in 1958, the chairman, Victor Sylvester, resigned. Letters between Sylvester and Cyril at that time reflect their good friendship. Sylvester pointed out that he could no longer devote the time for the chairman's duties and thanked Cyril for his great help. Cyril mentioned Sylvester's commitments to the Rank management and to his own orchestra, and said how much the ISTD would 'miss your inspiring leadership; your impartiality and willingness always to hear both sides of a case and your constant endeavour to find a just verdict'. Cyril was to continue the same policy during his own twelve years as chairman. When he retired in 1970, he said that he had

> not sought to be all things to all Branches, that would be too much to attempt. But I have tried to serve all Branches impartially and irrespective of size and influence. It gave me particular pleasure when I was a guest at a Ballroom Branch dinner to hear Mr [Alex] Moore state that I had the support of the Ballroom Branch.

Lightening the tone, he went on:

> Another thing which impressed me greatly was the way in which, during the Second World War, our examiners conducted examinations both in and away from London undeterred by air raids and transport difficulties. The watchword was: The Imperial must continue to function.

Cyril's letter to the Leslies in February 1959 included the news that 'the Dancers' Circle are proposing to give a dinner in my honour on April 12. I shall be the first writer and critic to be so honoured.' This delightful evening duly took place at the Savoy Hotel and was reported in *The Dancing Times* in May. Sacheverell Sitwell took the chair, and the toast was proposed by the eminent dance critic A.V. Coton. He spoke of Cyril's long list of publications, singling out four books – the *Complete Book*, the translation of Noverre's Letters, the study of Fokine and the Cecchetti Manual – any one of which would establish his 'lasting fame'. Ashton reminisced lightheartedly about his first meetings, 'as a schoolboy', with Cyril and Alice, and Marie Rambert joined the others in gratitude for his historical studies and his willingness to help artists with advice. Other people who spoke included Richard Buckle, Francis Mason (then cultural attaché at the American Embassy) and Peggy van Praagh, while telegrams were read from Ninette de Valois, Margaret Craske, Adeline Genée, Alicia Markova and Alexandra Danilova. Cyril replied, and Svetlana Beriosova presented him with a book of signatures.

Cyril's last review for the *Sunday Times* appeared on 23 August 1959. An editorial note said that he was retiring, and introduced his successor, Richard Buckle, who 'throughout his association with the world of dancing has received unstinted help and encouragement from Mr Beaumont'. Cyril's review covered a performance of the Royal Ballet's *Pineapple Poll*, carping a little about David Blair having become 'something of a languid, heavy swell, accepting female admiration as his due rather than a nuisance'. His dancing, however, was as neat, as lively and as infectious as ever. In Peter Wright's *A Blue Rose* he praised Anne Heaton and Donald MacLeary in the *pas de deux* of unrequited love, the two-step by Clover Roope and Michael Boulton, and 'the sharp-edged Tango of Boulton and Audrey Farriss, half Cretan amazon and half Black Queen'.

In a December 1959 letter to the Leslies, Cyril responded to 'the exciting news that you hope to make the long hoped-for trip to Europe next year'. He mentioned that he was keeping well, but that Alice was very hampered by arthritis, which gave her a great deal of pain. In his unpublished memoirs, Serge Leslie takes up the story of this important friendship. 'To arrive in London is always an experience but for us nothing but meeting the Beaumonts again mattered. The smiles of greeting and the inner warmth told us all was well.' Having travelled by sea, they could stay only for about two weeks, but after that they visited every four years. Serge was taken to see the present whereabouts of the London Archives of the Dance (it had been moved into the basement of the ISTD building in Gloucester Place) and was distressed to realise how little support for Cyril's dream had emerged from dancers and dance organisations.

In October 1960 *The Dancing Times* marked its fiftieth anniversary. Various writers contributed short pieces on great ballerinas from Genée (Ivor Guest) to Fonteyn (James Monahan). Cyril, however, covered the male dancers of the fifty years. An editorial note pointed out that in every case 'he writes about dancers as they appeared to him when they first danced their famous roles'. He began with Mordkin and how he danced to the pulsating throb of Glazunov's music in *Autumn Bacchanale*, and went on to Bolm, who excelled in character roles, and inevitably to Nijinsky, who had the rare gift of creating a completely different character with each change of role. Nicholas Kremneff and Leon Woizikowski were two outstanding character dancers, and Idzikowski had unusual technique and exceptional elevation. Massine was praised for a concentrated sense of theatre and absorption in his role, Dolin for his outstanding creations in *Le Train bleu* and *Job*, and Lifar for his superb rendering of *The Prodigal Son*. Jean Borlin was included, along with Eglevsky (in *L'Épreuve d'amour*), Orloff, Zoritch, and Rostov with the de Basil Ballet. Then, not surprisingly, there were tributes to Babilée and Petit, Kalioujny, Skouratoff and Skibine. Seven Danish dancers were listed, headed by Bruhn and Kronstam, while Fadeyechev and Lapauri were mentioned with the Bolshoi. Turning to Britain, he wrote about Helpmann's dramatic triumphs in *Apparitions*, *Hamlet* and de Valois's *Don Quixote*, of Turner's Blue Skater, of Somes, Gore, Alexander Grant, Gilpin and David Blair, among others. From America he selected Youskevitch (superlatively graceful), Kriza, Magallanes, Hugh Laing and Robbins. He summed up by saying that his choices were for those

who have moved me most, either by their interpretation of a

role, their evocation of a mood or for their sheer beauty of line and movement in an abstract work. Technical fireworks may delight for the moment but such efforts do not persist in the mind unless they stem from and contribute to the action.

Spring 1961 saw the beginning of a combined opus between Cyril and Serge Leslie, *A Bibliography of the Dance Collection of Doris Niles and Serge Leslie*, annotated by Leslie and edited by Cyril. Collecting and bibliographical research had initiated the friendship, and their mutual interest never faltered. On their first meeting, according to Leslie,

> the conversation turned to his [Cyril's] *Bibliography of Dancing* published in 1922 [*sic*; actually published 1929] (a small sensible book with a red buckram binding and beveled edges). It was (as were so many of Cyril's books) the first of its kind. Cyril explained the difficulties in assembling and cataloguing dance books and libretti as there had been no earlier work to guide him. I might have thought at this very moment that I would also be a bibliographer, for he impressed upon me the difficulties and necessity for correct and accurate descriptions of binding, size, paper, conditions etc. before passing on to the book's contents. Thus, in our earliest meetings, Cyril had changed the course of my thinking and collecting.

Now the major Niles–Leslie Collection was to be recorded in two successive volumes and a cumulative index of the published bibliography.

In an October 1962 letter, Cyril told Serge that, as the Cecchetti Society had been rearranging their examination grades, his three Primers had also to be rearranged. The printers had held him up time and time again. He was worried about the London County Council's plan to demolish in about two years' time the part of Charing Cross Road in which the shop was located. Good news, however, was that he had been awarded an OBE (Officer of the Order of the British Empire) and he had been to Buckingham Palace to receive it. (At that time Honours List awards for the performing arts were far less frequent, and therefore more of a distinction, than they became later.) As well as awarding the Légion d'Honneur, France had given him in 1934 the Palmes académiques. In 1962 he was created a Knight-Officer of the Order of Merit (Italy), and was also a Fellow of the Royal Society of Arts and a Fellow of the Royal Society of Literature. The dance world had recognised him with the Queen Elizabeth II Coronation Award of the Royal Academy of Dance and the Imperial Award of the ISTD. However, no British honorary doctorate ever came his way.

It was in 1963 that seventeen-year-old Leslie Getz from California came to London and, like so many others over the years, found her way to the shop. As a collector of dance books from the age of eleven, she had already been buying books from him by mail, but she was shy of identifying herself to him. Before she could do so, however, she was invited into his sanctum and later became one of his regular teatime callers. He proved to be a guide and mentor for her on ballet generally and collecting books in particular; she has amassed a major private dance library and edits the bibliographic guide to dance *Attitudes & Arabesques*. Her memories of Cyril are warm and appreciative:

> It became one of the cornerstones of my dance education, all those times of just sitting and talking… everyone would just talk. The whole ambience was one of a love of dance and people exchanging experiences and impressions.

She was amazed at his low-key, unassuming personality and his formal style: 'he was completely a creature of the Victorian era… to the point that to his last days he wore Victorian winged collars'. From him she learned not only about dance books but also about specialist periodicals and their value to researchers. 'He helped everyone in the most open-handed manner. If you demonstrated a serious interest, he would go to any length to be of help to you. Without question he was as great a person as he was a historian.'

But the days of the shop were now numbered. Cyril decided to sell, and in November 1965 he wrote to the Leslies describing the last days:

> The long negotiations about the shop came to a head in September [1964], and I agreed to vacate the premises at 75 on October 29. It has taken five weeks' hard work to move and clear 55 years' accumulation of books and papers. Although Jill Anne [Bowden] helped me, and some friends, the sorting out was a terrible job. The more books I got rid of the more there seemed to remain. We cleared four large motor van loads and several car loads. Some books I sold to booksellers, some to private people, and some were sent to Allstorage. Some I left here [68 Bedford Court Mansions] and others have been stored by friends. All this time I had to neglect correspondence and orders.

One of the friends who helped Cyril at this time was George Sims, who wrote about it later in the *London Magazine*. Sims had known him and the shop since the late 1940s, when he was starting up as a book dealer, and was particularly interested in the publications of the Beaumont Press. From 1963 onward he bought valuable manuscript and proof material of these publications from Cyril. Then, when Cyril was clearing out in 1965, '[he] asked me to go to No 75 and help sort out the books in the cellar. Due to bomb damage… the premises had been damaged below the ground floor and this added to the general mess and confusion.' One of the finds 'was an unopened parcel dating from 1910 containing a dozen copies of the first edition of H.G. Wells's novel *The History of Mr Polly*. Sims later visited Cyril privately, buying some things he had decided to sell: 'His wife was an invalid for many years, cared for in St George's Nursing Home, and the expense of this had to be met somehow after he retired.' (In fact, Alice was in and out of many nursing homes, but it may be credited to Cyril's attentive care that she outlived him by seven months to the day, dying on 24 December 1976.)

In spite of closing the shop, Cyril had plenty with which to occupy his time. In May 1966 G.B.L. Wilson wrote in *The Dancing Times* that he had visited the Beaumonts' flat and found him 'surrounded by treasures, one of which is a superb drawing by Picasso of Lopokova. He recalled Diaghilev's visits to the bookshop with Nijinsky.' This flat is described in extraordinary detail by Serge Leslie. You entered 'down a narrow corridor with walls choc à bloc (as the British say) with framed pictures, engravings and lithographs relating to the dance.' You then went into the drawing room, full of things to look at: a monogrammed chocolate service made in Vienna for Napoleon's personal use; a statuette of Emma Livry in *Le Papillon*; rare nineteenth-century paintings and lithographs of dancers, including one of Perrot giving a class at the Paris Opéra; a 'stunning' photograph of Nijinsky in *Le Spectre de la rose*; a bronze of Bolm in *Prince Igor*. Original costumes of Nijinsky, Bolm, and others were stored in cardboard boxes. The Picasso drawing was cherished, and Cyril worried about it to the extent of slipping it at times under the corner of a large rug…. 'After his passing an inventory was taken, and it was missing from the wall. Only after a delay of several days was it found. It seems he had not confided the location of its hide-out to anyone.'

Two items that reflected daily life are also mentioned: on a buffet 'was a collection of sherries for guests, as Cyril might occasionally drink a glass of wine, but in the main was most abstemious'. Not only was he a rare wine drinker, he knew little about wine – George Sims records that there were many bottles, presents from visitors, standing upright in the kitchen; Cyril had no idea that wines should lie on their sides. There was also a television set – he relaxed with certain British comedy series and American Western films. Nancy Bowden later wrote in *The Dancing Times* that as a viewer 'he had a taste for individual artistry, from the expressive intensity of the late James Dean to the comic presence and consummate timing of Frankie Howerd'. His reading, she recorded, was varied and extensive: 'although he prefers prose, he has pleasure in verse, particularly in the dramas of Shakespeare and the poetry of John Clare. But his greatest interests, apart from ballet, are military history and period uniforms.'

One of Cyril's unfulfilled intentions was to write a biography of Marie Taglioni, and for many years he had collected information and memorabilia with that in view. His interest had been stimulated when he met Margaret Rolfe, who, as a child, had known and been taught by Taglioni when she lived in London. Rolfe called in to the shop to ask whether he knew what had happened to some Taglioni souvenirs that she had given to Pavlova and he was able to tell her that when Pavlova died they had been handed on to the Archives Internationales de la Danse in Paris. This did not please Rolfe, who had hoped they would remain in Britain; but this meeting began a friendship between Cyril and Margaret, who showed him, among other things, an exercise book she had kept about Taglioni. On one of the pages was the recipe for a particular seed cake, which

Taglioni loved and the Rolfe family always made for her. Cyril, remembering how Drury Lane Theatre celebrated Twelfth Night with a Baddeley Cake, named after the eighteenth-century actor Robert Baddeley, told de Valois of the Taglioni recipe and together they decided to initiate an annual Taglioni Cake ceremony for the Royal Ballet. Starting on 22 June 1957, this took place on the last day of the ballet season in the greenroom at Covent Garden between the matinee and evening performances. Each year the cake was cut by a distinguished guest or a retiring dancer, with Markova the first of a celebrated list.

Serge Leslie describes items of the Rolfe Taglioni Collection, which Cyril showed him in 1969. They included watercolour drawings and paintings made by Margaret of Taglioni's activities and classes. These she had cut out and made into a collage on large sheets of matt black paper. One of them showed pupils in a social dance, *Le Coussin*, in which one male dancer was high-kicking while two couples performed other steps. Leslie goes on:

> One day Cyril again produced one of his memorable surprises. In his quiet and effective manner he presented Doris [Niles] with the following: first, a tiny green leather almanac (nicely stamped in gold), a solid gold button hook which Taglioni used… finally, the earrings which Taglioni wore in *La Bayadère* [*Le Dieu et la Bayadère*]. They were lovely graded balls of deep blue cloisonné with small brilliants which flashed as the dancer moved… Years later, when Marcia Haydée and the Stuttgart Ballet made their last appearance in Los Angeles, Doris presented these items to her.

In *The Dancing Times* of September 1966, Cyril wrote an article on other Taglioni treasures as a result of meeting a direct descendant of Marie's brother Paul, the Princess Mary

Windisch-Graetz. She showed him a set of costume designs for Paul Taglioni ballets, five of which were reproduced with his article. A second piece dealt with some recently discovered portraits of the Taglioni family found in a private collection in Vienna. They were of Filippo, Marie, Paul, his wife Amalie (all by Friedrich Wilhelm Herdt) and Paul's daughter Marie the Younger (by Alexius Canzi). The Theatre Museum of London now has a number of mementoes of Marie Taglioni left to them by Cyril, including personal possessions such as a needlework box, doll's house accessories, purses, shoes and fans. Another Taglioni treasure surfaced in 1973. G.B.L. Wilson reported in his *Dancing Times* column how the dancer Brenda Hamlyn had bought from an antique shop run in Camden Passage by another former dancer, Sara Luzita, an ebony and gold necklace to which was attached a note saying that it had once belonged to Taglioni. Hamlyn took it to show Cyril, who confirmed that the handwriting on the note was that of Margaret Rolfe. One precious souvenir was given to Cyril by Rolfe in 1952. A tiny letter from her reads:

> Having wrestled with myself for years, I have at last decided to give you a minute gold locket containing the hair of Marie Taglioni, who had four of these lockets made, and these she presented to Carlotta Grisi, Fanny Cerrito, Lucile Grahn, keeping one for herself. They were given as keepsakes at Her Majesty's Theatre, July 12, 1845, on the occasion when the celebrated *Pas de Quatre* was danced there. This locket I am giving to you was the one she had made for herself and which years after she gave to my grandmother as a keepsake.

However, the locket is not among the Taglioni items in the Theatre Museum.

When William Beaumont Morris, an Australian-born longtime friend and often helper in the shop, died on 14 August 1966, Cyril contributed a long obituary of him to *The Dancing Times*. Most of us knew Montie, and Cyril describes him with affectionate accuracy:

A slim, frail elderly man over the statutory three score years and ten, with pale, clean-shaven features crowned with a thinning, unruly crest of white hair, his counterpart might well be found among the portraits by Phiz. His manner varied between the shy and the warm-hearted, almost effusive. He had a lively sense of humour and delighted in retailing items of gossip – never unkind... [His love of the theatre] had invested him with a slightly theatrical air. I always recall his walk when leaving 75 to go home. He would clap on his beret, give it a Beatty tilt, and with a swing of the hips saunter out with a jaunty stride, like a light comedian making his exit from on stage.

Cyril described what a keen hunter Montie was for collecting everything connected with the Diaghilev Ballet – he had even found a very rare copy of the issue of the *Annals of the Imperial Theatres* edited by Diaghilev and inscribed with his signature. He summed up with the words, 'No one could wish for a better or more faithful friend... he was loyalty and generosity personified.'

During 1967 and 1968, *The Dancing Times* published occasional articles by Cyril, mostly on historical subjects. In March 1967, under the title *Musings from near the Museum*, he wrote about another Taglioni memento, a dressmaker's model made to her measurements and kept in her dressing room, and about Cléo de Mérode's memoirs, *Le Ballet de Ma Vie* (she had just died, aged ninety-one, in Paris). In August 1967 his article was about Katti Lanner's National Training School for Dancing, founded in 1876. In the *Museum Musings* in November he discussed male dancers of the past and also wrote about Rosita Mauri. In August 1968, under the title *Dancers in Unexpected Places*, he revealed another of his current interests, tracking down 'articles designed specifically to appeal to the general public seeking a remembrance of a dancer whose art had aroused their admiration'. Charmingly illustrated, this dealt with such delightful objects as mantel clocks with figures from *La Sylphide* or *Le Dieu et la Bayadère*, a bronze candelabrum of Fanny Elssler in her Cachucha, a double brass plaque of her in two roles, the Cachucha and *La Gypsy*, and boxes of paper dolls of Taglioni or Elssler with changes of costumes.

When Serge Grigoriev died on 28 August 1968, Cyril wrote a long appreciation in *The Dancing Times* of the man he had known well. True to his own style, Cyril included a physical description:

> He was unusually tall, dark and spare, his thinning hair brushed close to his head. He was clean shaven, with rather sad eyes, and a serious intellectual expression which could soften into a charming smile. Normally he spoke softly, his speech being slightly sibilant. He was impartial, brisk in manner, and business-like in all his dealings... Occasionally something might annoy him and then he would raise his clenched hands above his head and shake them furiously.

Cyril remained actively concerned with the ISTD and the Cecchetti Society. In December 1968, when he wrote to Serge Leslie, he mentioned 'many things to do for the Imperial Society':

> The Society has taken over the London College of Dance

and Drama and it has been quite a business to find suitable premises in which to house it. But at last we found a School in Marylebone Lane which is quite large and was about to be vacated, and of course it has had to be cleared and washed and reorganised to suit the new requirements. This College is, I think, so far as this country is concerned, the only one to be devoted to the training of teachers of dancing.

A coda to this turned up in *The Dancing Times* seven months later when the Dance and Drama College celebrated its Silver Anniversary at the Café Royal. Cyril had spoken about the negotiations for the premises: 'The building was formerly a boys' school, and Mr Beaumont's dry account of how certain sanitary arrangements had to be altered had everyone roaring with laughter.'

In the December 1968 letter to the Leslies, Cyril added that negotiations with the Victoria and Albert Museum had also been practically completed, 'and so the London Archives of the Dance has been transferred there – quite a job'. Alice, although very much an invalid, had been 'working on a little item of needlework for you both. It is quite different in style from the other you have had, and is intended as a centrepiece for your table when you have a celebration tea.' When they were in London the Leslies always went to Cecchetti Society Demonstrations, and in July 1969 one of these was held in Bloomsbury, when Fonteyn was present. According to Leslie,

> No matter how many distinguished guests or artists appeared, the light of Cyril Beaumont shone like a beacon, and all gravitated towards him. One had only to see him, impeccably clothed in tuxedo or full [evening] dress – usually with a boutonniere – signing programmes for enthralled students, being photographed with celebrities, or speaking from the

Cyril with Doris Niles and Serge Leslie at a Cecchetti Demonstration.

stage, to feel the tremendous cohesion this quiet figure managed to form about him.

Cyril's caring interest for young dancers was constantly manifested. As often happens, a man with no children of his own and a teacher manqué was able to stretch out a helping hand to other people's children. He related extremely well to the students of the Cecchetti Society and of other dance schools. Nesta Brooking knew him in both capacities. At the Cecchetti Society, she and Diana Barker were willingly roped in by him to prepare a little box of chocolates for each pupil gaining grade certificates at the annual presentations. The boxes were rectangular, coloured a pretty shade of pink, and each bore a special cover label of Schwabe's portrait of the seated Maestro Cecchetti. Nesta and Diana bought exactly the kind of assorted chocolates he wanted, placed them carefully – two soft-centred, two hard-centred, two nut-filled, and so on – in each box and tied round it a matching pink satin ribbon cut to a length that allowed a neat bow on top. Cyril then handed one out with each certificate, and the receiving girl would bob him a curtsey in thanks. At Nesta's own school he often talked to the students about ballet history and great dancers. He also decided that they should be encouraged to express themselves in writing essays, not just about ballet but about anything they had found interesting – a holiday or a family outing, a book or a performance. Helped by Nancy Bowden, he read all the entries and wrote comments.

Another obituary, contributed to *The Dancing Times* in August 1969, was of A.V. Coton, who, Cyril wrote, was deservedly regarded as one of our leading ballet critics. He had 'attained that position solely by hard work over many years, and a dogged determination to succeed. He had always had a deep love for the performing arts, his chief concern being that of the ballet.' Cyril then reminisced about how, from the 1930s, Coton would come to see him at the shop and they would discuss new ballet productions or a rising dancer of promise. Again, there was a personal portrait:

> He was strongly built and radiated personality. He had an unusually large head and broad brow… He did not suffer fools gladly and he could be brusque on occasion. But, speaking personally, I always found him a delightful companion with a lively sense of humour… The Royal Opera House audience on ballet nights will not seem the same, lacking that long familiar dominating figure, that masterful tread, and the leonine head, slightly tilted, as though to catch a stray whisper of news borne on the quivering warm air.

In July 1970 Cyril resigned from the chairmanship of the ISTD, but he continued his work for the Cecchetti Society. He still found, recommended and sometimes acquired rare books for the Leslies to add to their collection. Leslie records that Cyril now had fewer offers of books, as 'runners' preferred to go to shops that would pay higher prices. He quotes Cyril as saying that 'he no longer went to Sotheby sales, as the prices were fierce (a word that was awesome in his vocabulary)'. He did, however, come up with some special finds, either of books or lithographs. Most of his letters to Leslie in the 1970s deal with tracing copies of books, sometimes for friends of the Leslies. In 1973 he found copies of Beaumont Press books, including a book on *Robert Lloyd, The Actor* with a preface by Edmund Blunden that was in the Press format but not one of the Press series. Other books mentioned are an edition of *Les Très Riches Heures du Duc de Berry*, Roy Strong's *Splendour at Court: Renaissance Spectacle and Illusion* and Charles Spencer's *Léon Bakst*.

The resignation from the ISTD was marked by a dinner in his honour at the Park Lane Hotel on 29 November 1970, and *The Dancing Times* included a report. Alex Moore of the ISTD was in the chair and de Valois gave the first speech, speaking of Cyril's great integrity as a critic and also of the institution of the Taglioni Cake ceremony. Richard Buckle followed with 'a very sympathetic account of Mr Beaumont, the great scholar and writer whose number of publications nearly equalled the years since he first saw Pavlova dance at the Palace Theatre'. Buckle mentioned Cyril's writings for *Ballet* and that he had advanced money for the magazine on 'generous (but businesslike) terms'. Beryl Grey then proposed Cyril's health and unveiled a portrait of him by Rupert Shephard.

Cyril's reply appeared in ISTD's *Dance Journal*. He sketched the Society's development since 1904: it now had eight thousand members and eleven different branches covering different techniques. In 1924 they had extended to include ballroom dancing, and one of their presidents had been Victor Sylvester. Sylvester, said Cyril,

> was, and to some of us still is, the Prince Charming of Ballroom Dancing. But the charm masks an alert brain and a shrewd man of affairs, sharpened by close attention to physical fitness. Even today, he skips daily and has weekly workouts in a gymnasium. Can he be contemplating a challenge to Henry Cooper [one of Britain's most successful and popular pugilists]?

He mentioned the books that he had encouraged the Society to publish, such as Melusine Wood's treatises on Historical Dance, and Joan Lawson's translations of Russian descriptions of folk and character dances.

In January 1971 there was a domestic note in Cyril's letter to Leslie because of the power cuts just before Christmas:

> We were not too badly off for heat, as our fire and our cooker are both gas which was not affected. But we had some cuts in electric light and as this happens without warning it can be dangerous, for instance if you happen to be in the lift. One morning I had to shave by the light of a single candle, which was tricky with the flame waving in the draught. We spent a very quiet Christmas and I managed to cope with the cooking which worked out well, after juggling with the burners. One always seems to want more burners than one has.

Another strike was mentioned in March:

> As a result of the Post Office strike we have been unable to receive or send any letters. At first it was rather pleasant to let the world go by; no letters, no bills, even tax demands held up. Then it became irritating, because one was waiting for replies on various subjects.

In the same letter he wrote of a new development in his life:

I don't know if I mentioned it before, but some of our Cecchetti Group had the charming thought of recording on tape the speeches at the [ISTD] Dinner so that Alice could hear them as delivered. About a week ago, a deputation of two arrived with a recorder and tapes, and Alice was able to hear the speeches quite well. I was presented with the tapes, and if you have a recorder or I can borrow one you will be able to hear them.

This led to more recording. According to Leslie's memoirs, the New York Public Library sent an interviewer to record Cyril's voice relating various facts about his life and publications. Then, when Serge and Doris were living in London, Cyril did a series of recordings for them, each section prefaced by an introduction by Doris. In the first of these, he read a speech about Cecchetti that he gave at the Golden Jubilee of the Cecchetti Society, which was celebrated on 24 July 1972 with another dinner at the Park Lane Hotel. The two awards, the Cecchetti Society Choreographic Competition and the Cyril Beaumont Award for a Cecchetti student at the Royal Ballet School, continued annually. Cyril usually attended, and often made the presentations. He had already appeared on television, contributing to programmes about Diaghilev in 1968, a 1970 Pavlova programme, speaking of her season at the Palace Theatre and the famous 'Mordkin slap', and in 1973 one on Massine.

The third part of the Niles–Leslie Bibliography was published in 1973, but domestic matters dominated Cyril's letters to them about that Christmas. Alice was in a nursing home, so the Bowdens had Christmas dinner with him at home. He visited Alice in the morning, and had to take taxis (very expensive) both ways. 'Our capon cooked very well and was most tender', but there was a disaster with the Christmas pudding. It was supposed to be heated in a steamer but he did not have one. He put it into a basin of hot water,

> but the bottom of the basin melted and the contents acquired an undesirable and unexpected addition. However, a search of my store cupboard revealed a jar of mincemeat which seemed quite all right, although aspersions were cast upon its age – comparable to the Pyramids! – and we made a mincemeat tart which was much appreciated.

In February 1974 he was able to report to Leslie that he had traced a copy of the lithograph of *Le Pas des Déesses*, the rarest of the Romantic Ballet lithographs. It was 'quite a nice print' and the price was £200. He was far from well that spring, and eventually his doctor suggested that he should go to Torquay for a rest. This meant a four-hour train journey, but he stayed in a hotel from which he could see the harbour and watch sailing vessels. The weather was warm and he was able to sit out among Torquay's well-known semi-tropical flowers and trees. Soon he was eating better, and able to enjoy coach drives to Dartmoor and Plymouth.

In February 1975 he contributed what proved to be his last article to *The Dancing Times*. It was about *Cartophily applied to dancers*, cartophily being the collecting of cigarette cards, and he described a German book of the 1930s, *Der Künstlerische Tanz*, which dealt with thirteen sets of cigarette cards relating to dance. Dancers and choreographers illustrated represented world-renowned dancers (such as Pavlova, Karsavina and Isadora Duncan), German free dance, German stage dancing, Viennese dance, Russian dance, Spanish dance, French and Italian dance, Nordic dance, Oriental dance and German schools of dance. As Cyril commented, 'The choice of dancers to represent a particular country or dance form occasionally verges on the absurd.' The choice for England included Dolin, Wendy Toye and Derra de Moroda, but omitted de Valois, Markova and Rambert. American dance included Martha Graham, Agnes de Mille and Ted Shawn, but not Ruth St Denis. Russia had by far the best selection, including Fokine, Spessiva, Bolm, Nijinska and Lifar.

Another seaside visit, this time to Bournemouth's Highcliff Hotel, was made in August. There he enjoyed 'a brilliant display of aero-acrobatics with beautiful changes of formation' by the Red Devils. He browsed through antique shops and bookshops, which had 'nothing in the really rare range', and also enjoyed the Russell-Coles Museum, which had a bust of his greatly admired Napoleon and a table the Emperor had used on St. Helena, as well as a large collection of material about Sir Henry Irving.

Cyril was now working on a new book, *Bookseller at the Ballet*, which brought together in chronological order material from his earlier *Flashback* and *The Diaghilev Ballet in London* plus more autobiographical memories. In the end it went only as far as 1929. Leslie and the editorially experienced Jill Anne Bowden helped with the index. All three got together in Cyril's kitchen, where there was a suitable long table for proofs, record cards, reference books and a typewriter. Cyril and Leslie sat facing each other and Cyril called out the item for Leslie to type on a card. It was a nine-to-five task for a number of weeks. Each day Cyril prepared lunch, frequently lamb chops and potatoes, followed by a custard pudding. After the book was published, Serge and Cyril parcelled out complimentary and review copies. Leslie described this activity:

> Cyril had developed a rather unusual method of wrapping his books. Using newspaper under a stiff, rough paper, he managed to fashion four protruding corners which absorbed

the shock which packages are subject to by the postal service. He had very strong hands, a pianist's hands actually. I could not quite make the packages to his standard and so my role consisted of loading them into a small cart and escorting them to the post office.

The Cecchetti Society launched *Bookseller at the Ballet* with a large lunch reception on 26 November at the Coliseum Theatre, with speeches by Sacheverell Sitwell, Michael Wood (director of the Royal Ballet School) and Laura Wilson. It was, of course, reviewed in the dance journals. Mary Clarke, in *The Dancing Times*, began nostalgically:

> Twenty years ago a group of writers on ballet played a game in which you had to choose the one book you would like to take to your desert island and justify your choice. An easy winner was Cyril Beaumont's *The Diaghilev Ballet in London…* because of all his books – and in those days we were almost dependent on Mr Beaumont for scholarly works on ballet – it was the most personal.

She was delighted that *The Diaghilev Ballet in London*, long out of print, had now been incorporated into *Bookseller at the Ballet*. She pointed out that generations of dancers and dance lovers had called at the shop and known Mr Beaumont and 'every single one of them will want his book'.

Cyril, as always eminently realistic, wrote to the Leslies in January 1976 that

> there was a splendid notice in *The Dancing Times* for January, which should help, and I understand there are to be notices in *Dance and Dancers* and *Dance Gazette*. I think it is a good time to be among the Christmas books; on the other hand there are so many to be reviewed that the notices are short,

and it takes time for reviews to appear and not to be elbowed out because space is precious.

Peter Williams wrote the review in *Dance and Dancers*, which began, 'Cyril Beaumont has no need to go digging; he was there when most of it happened.' And of the shop, he wrote,

> I find it sad, walking down Charing Cross Road today, that number 75 has not been preserved as an historical monument since so much dance history originated from [it]. It is good to know that at least it lives on, together with the famous and infamous characters who visited it, in Cyril Beaumont's autobiography.

On publication day, seven Royal Ballet School students from White Lodge (Elizabeth Griffiths, Angela Cox, Lucy Bethune, Susan Holden, Andris Plucis, Matthew Hawkins and Andrew Ward) took copies of the book to his book-signing session at Dance Books to be signed for the school library. That week the Ballet Section of the Critics' Circle (Cyril had been president of the Critics' Circle in 1957) also gave him a luncheon at which Oleg Kerensky and Matthew Norgate were the speakers.

Although he was well, and able to enjoy these events, only a short time remained to Cyril after *Bookseller at the Ballet* was published. Leslie remembers that the spring of 1976 was cold, rainy and penetrating. He met Cyril regularly at the tube station nearest to his own flat [Earls Court] and they 'would share the journey and packages to Redcliffe Gardens':

> This was the period he was bringing me treasures from his own collection: dozens of original Russian synopsii, many of them ballets of Petipa; various articles of his own that he had gone to much trouble to unearth, and sometimes a beautiful lithograph. Our apartment was warm and after resting for a

few moments in his large chair he would go to the kitchen to prepare scones to go with raspberry jam... When the weather was fierce, and I could see Cyril was tired, I would send him home in a taxi.

Leslie did not realise that Cyril was really ill until he received a letter from him, dated 7 April, saying that he had been taken to University College Hospital for tests. He was in hospital for two months, regularly visited by friends (I remember meeting Serge Leslie there when I went to see Cyril). There was a prostate operation, but on 24 May 1976, he died. His family and friends were at the burial at St Pancras Cemetery, beyond East Finchley, on 2 June; I recall being driven home by G.B.L. Wilson. Rather a long time later, on 11 August, a service of thanksgiving was held at St Paul's Church, Covent Garden. Sara Kestelman read *The Primrose Bank* by Cyril's favourite poet, John Clare, Nadia Nerina read an extract from *Bookseller at the Ballet*, Philip Gammon of the Royal Ballet's music staff played the finale from *L'Oiseau de feu*, de Valois spoke and various hymns were sung.

Obituaries appeared, the most perceptive, inevitably, from his fellow ballet critics. Looking through them, I find phrases I appreciate. David Dougill (*Sunday Times*) described him as 'the quiet oracle of British ballet'. One of the most charming, brief and beautifully worded tributes came from Alexander Bland (Nigel Gosling and Maude Lloyd) in *The Observer*:

> The absence henceforward from ballet occasions of the bristly, benevolent presence of Cyril Beaumont will leave a double gap. His death at 84 has removed an expert witness and recorder of the Diaghilev age and also a rare character – dedicated scholar and practical enthusiast, a kind, honest and gently amusing man. Affectionately mocked in middle age

for his prim though sharp-eyed style, he lived to find himself revered, as he deserved, as an authority.

Ivor Guest, very much the inheritor of his dedication to historical research, wrote in *Dance* that the dance world 'has lost one of its greatest figures', going on to say:

> Dance historians everywhere owe him a great debt. He was a pioneer in the truest sense, for little serious dance history – at least in English – had been published before he made his first appearance in print... As a practising historian, I find it salutary to reflect, not only how much I refer to Beaumont's books and how much I use them as springboards for more detailed investigation, but on their influence on me when I was turning to the study of the dance and its history.

He made another very valid point about Cyril's helpfulness that I have found echoed from practising artists and dance writers in every part of the world. When Guest was virtually unknown and showed him the typescript of his book on the Second Empire ballet, Cyril 'discussed it at great length, one chapter at a time, in the dark inner sanctum of his shop. This was, as I discovered, a typical example of his generosity, from which many, many others benefited too.'

Clive Barnes wrote equally warmly in the *New York Times*. Describing him as 'a man of enormous importance to all of us who are interested in dance', he continued,

> Criticism was not his major strength... Yet, as a historian, he is totally unmatched and unmatchable... Book after book came out, as he recorded ballets not just of his time but of history... It is a monumental compendium, for which he never received sufficient recognition in his lifetime... For much of his life he was an unknown worker in an unknown field... More than any other man, Beaumont made us aware

of ballet's past. I liked him very much and admired him enormously.

There was more than one opinion about Cyril as a critic, however. Clive Barnes's and Alexander Bland's views were not shared by Baird Hastings. In an article in *Ballet Review* about two very particular critics, he linked Beaumont and Lincoln Kirstein, 'a pair of paragons on a pedestal – two to believe'. His very perceptive comparison between the two men was carefully weighted and presented:

> Without the work of these two perceptive and literate critics I might never have begun to understand the aesthetics of the ballet. With differing intellects and differing instincts, they were both fearless informers.

He makes a fine assessment of Cyril as a writer:

> His guides to most ballets created during his entire period of activity are as fresh today as they were when they were first written. And in my experience they are so well written one sees the ballet unfold in front of one as one reads… His prose is colourful, effective, unobtrusive.

He sums up, 'Both these writers had God's gift of insight and ability to write accurate descriptions of what they saw and felt.'

In 1955 Mary Clarke had described very succinctly (in *Ballet – a Decade of Endeavour*) Cyril's unusually rock-solid approach to dance criticism. Although stylistic fashions changed, 'he writes on undisturbed', and she praised 'his unshakeable detachment, his refusal to gush' and 'his balanced and unexcitable judgements'. Katherine Adelman, in her 1982 thesis, felt that

> [he] was a critic in the most positive sense of the word. In every technique of examination he employed to study dance he produced original and provocative statements that

illuminated not only specific events but the art as a whole...
As a chronicler he recorded and recaptured a clear sense of
the ballet and the artistry of dancers he studied in detail,
providing useful documents for historians. As a visionary
exponent he increased understanding of the ballet medium
by clarifying the link between its artistic form and subject
matter and between dance and its sister arts, design and
music.

This man, who at first sight seems to be simplicity
personified, was in fact a many-layered personality of acute
perception and wide-ranging cultural interests. Contrasts and
diversity intrigued him – and it was because he found in the
stage dance of his time and its historical background immense
differences of styles, contexts and intentions that it became the
major part of his life's work. Associated in many people's minds
only with Diaghilev's Ballets Russes, his thoughts and emotions
were in fact equally devoted to innovative modern movements
in dance, to every form of non-ballet dance, to multimedia and
cinematic techniques and to puppet theatre. Indeed, for him
much of the fascination of Diaghilev's world was that it stretched
over the years from *Les Sylphides* and *Petrouchka* to *Les Biches*, *Les
Noces* and *Ode*; that it continually provided new experiences,
new music, new designs.

Beaumont's essential strength came from his stable
background, from the early training that led him to balance
science with art, and from the stimulating divergence of cultural
approach, part English, part French, engendered by his fluency in
both languages. To his analysis of dance productions he was able
to bring a valuable knowledge of history and literature, as well as
of music, design and acting. Keenly responsive to drama in plays
and ballets, sympathetic to the attitudes and problems of theatre
artists, his often-hidden but delightfully dry sense of humour

Cyril holding his Emma Livry statuette.

meant that he had no inclination to lead a histrionic personal life. Setting his artistic standards on the highest professional level, he was still in caring touch with the youngest pupils taking their first steps in a dance school show. Lacking false modesty, and secure in the good opinion of those he valued, he was free of petty jealousies and entirely unmotivated by the competitive ambition of a careerist. Never seeking the limelight, he was, all the same, articulate and positive whenever he had to stand centre stage.

Integrity of reactions and devoted scholarship earned for Beaumont the respect of the dance world, but its affection was compelled by the human warmth that characterised his dealings with other human beings. Behind the reticent façade that some shop customers remember, countless examples of personal kindness are on record: a long line of young men and women beginning careers as performing artists or hopeful writers were listened to, understood, advised, encouraged – and never forgotten. With those who came from abroad, correspondence went on, with exchanges of letters or telegrams, keeping in touch with ambitions, with activities, with relationships. They sent thanks for advice about new roles, for suggestions about artistic collaborators, over technical difficulties. He sent flowers for first nights, flowers for injured or sick dancers in hospital, congratulations for successes, sympathy for disappointments. We all knew that he was a friend to whom we could turn. So, over and above the imposing list of his publications, his solid contribution to ballet history and appreciation, this workaholic writer, researcher and publisher, this retiring man who travelled little, ended up with a worldwide network of fond and grateful friends.